MW01598967

North of California St.

North of California St.

Selected Poems 1975–1999

GEORGE STANLEY

Vancouver   New Star Books   2014

NEW STAR BOOKS LTD.
107 – 3477 Commercial Street
Vancouver, BC V5N 4E8   CANADA

1517 – 1574 Gulf Road
Point Roberts, WA 98281   USA

www.NewStarBooks.com
info@NewStarBooks.com

The publisher acknowledges the financial support of the Canada Council for the Arts, the Government of Canada through the Canada Book Fund, the British Columbia Arts Council, and the Government of British Columbia through and the Book Publishing Tax Credit.

Cataloguing information for this book is available from Library and Archives Canada, www.collectionscanada.gc.ca.

Cover design by Oliver McPartlin
Printed on 100% post-consumer recycled paper.
Printed and bound in Canada by Imprimerie Gauvin, Gatineau, QC
First printing, June 2014

Contents

Introduction: George Stanley's North
  by Sharon Thesen   vii

1

Icarus   3
Opening Day   4
San Francisco's Gone   9
San Jose Poem   29
Paradise Shelter   34
Raft   42
Mozart & Cold Cuts   44
Easter Sunday '75   47
Down in the Flats   49
Vancouver in April   50
Donatello's David   53
'Chateau Sleaze'   56
The Set   57
The Berlin Wall   59
Three Chinese Men   62
The End of Bohemia?   64
The Puck   65
After John Newlove   69
The City   70
Poem Enclosing its Dedications   73
The Young Monks Understand Eternity Better   75
Abner   77
Return of the Abbot   79
The Power of the Unhappy People   81
A Man   82
Outside the Kingdome   83
Sex at 62   84
Robson St. '97   86

2

Mountains & Air — 89
Gentle Northern Summer — 103
KAL 007 — 108
Pub Night — 111
Terrace '85 — 113
My New Past — 117
Terrace '87 — 119
Death Thing — 123
For Prince George — 126
Teenage Boredom Poem — 127
The Hangover — 129
Spring '90 — 131
Terrace Landscapes — 132
Union Hall — 153
A Trip in Ireland — 154
Arklow — 156
Coolgreany — 157
The Void — 159
The Aanme — 160
Terrace '79 — 164
In Scotland — 166
In Ireland — 167
At Andy's — 169

INTRODUCTION

George Stanley's North

by Sharon Thesen

The phrase "North of California St." appears in the epigraph to George Stanley's long poem "San Francisco's Gone," written while he was living in Terrace, BC. The city of his birth, San Francisco was also the location of his coming-of-age as a poet, a gay poet, a student of Jack Spicer, and a member of the San Francisco Renaissance cohort that included Robert Duncan and Robin Blaser. Stanley's epigraph acknowledges a high-school poetry teacher, Edward Dermott 'Ned' Doyle, who first introduced him to poetry and, ultimately, to what he would find by travelling "north of California St." — that is, the rest of his life in poetry, the life that meant "breaking away" from his family. San Francisco being "gone" alludes in part to the fire that consumed the city in 1906, a catastrophe that still dwells in Stanley's ancestral memory; but also to a loss of its personal meaning and specific vitality, its old progressivism and bohemianism. This poem's vivid, prose-stanza composition coincides with a poetic practice that Stanley was developing while living and working in Terrace, BC, a place that radically continued the "north" trajectory of that original crossing of California St. at age 23.

North of California St. is a new volume assembled from the contents of four earlier, out-of-print, mostly New Star books. Not so much a career retrospective as a retrospective reading of these four books — *Opening Day* (1983, Oolichan Books); *Temporarily* (1985, a Gorse-Tatlow chapbook); *Gentle Northern Summer* (1995); and *At Andy's* (2000) — *North of California St.* presents the poems in the order of the three locations corresponding to Stanley's move north from San Francisco to Vancouver in 1971, and then another five hundred miles north, by air, from Vancouver to Terrace in 1976. As Stanley observes in the poem "A Trip in Ireland," "Time doesn't all run one way. Time, too, has a geography, has caves." While each of the four original books contains poems about all three places, this volume demonstrates the vision emerging as Stanley's earlier condensed lyric style was being supplanted by a more exigent and expansive one. Style in this book replaces temporality both in order of composition and order of experience, itself a possibility of style. The new and dynamic life conditions of the Terrace years provoked innovations and compositional methods that would continue to be developed and refined in the books Stanley has published since 2000, *Vancouver: A Poem* (2008) and *After Desire* (2013).

What was it about Terrace that led Stanley into writing some of the most beautiful and affecting poetry of our time — poems such as the sublime "Veracruz", as well as some of the most culturally and politically astute, such as "Terrace Landscapes"? In the two decades corresponding to Stanley's living and working there, approximately the mid-1970s to the mid-1990s, post-structuralist theory and language-centred writing (which had a strong base in San Francisco) were claiming the territory of effective cultural and political critique for themselves alone. A language-centred poetics driven by critical discourse provided younger avant-garde writers with a methodology that separated them from the late modernism of the 1960s and 1970s and its remnants of romanticism and expressionist politics. Part of what George Stanley's poetry is about is the difficulty—in life and in poetry—of separating secularism from cosmology, and perception from presence. In "The Set," a poem about Vancouver in the early 1970s, Stanley asks, "Do you miss ... that sense there was a world & meaning / outside your mind?"

> *Tho skeptic Ed Dorn*
> *said 'the set,' you could account*
> *not just for the world but for nature itself:*
> *the trees that leafed in the spring on Powell St.*

the stars — for you thought,
why would there be stars if there were
no world for them to shine on?

In *North of California St.*, Stanley's poetry struggles for the real, the world, and the person (not the past) against what critic Paul Virilio sees as the "pure war" conditions of virtuality, atopia, and globalization. Few poets have written with such clarity about conditions that are now ubiquitous. The fallen in this "pure war," such as the homeless young people on Vancouver's Granville Mall, have failed the imperative to "compete, compute, consume," neoliberalism's marching orders as alliterated by Stanley. Traditional preoccupations of war poetry — death, youth, desire, elegy, tenderness — haunt these poems. "Terrace Landscapes" temporalizes geography by bringing the Gulf War into Terrace's colonized past, its resource-extracted present further colonized by what Virilio calls the "globalization of affects". Talking about the Gulf War (a war famously without images) in one of his English classes, Stanley finds himself "in the thick,"

in thickets of discourses, prompted by the students, the techie
discourse, the geopolitical, the petroleum, the ecology, what
of the monsoons? I'm shifting, no, turning, from one to the
other, to each person, with her questions, & all the discourses
together make a fabric, a textile, something to wrap us in —

This sense of urgency and emergence contributes to this volume's essayistic voice and appearance on the page, and enhances by contrast the interiority and physical beauty of the lineated poems' presence on the page, their lucid and delighting diction. Stanley's work embeds all these qualities in every poem — from "Return of the Abbot" to "Berlin Wall" to "The Power of the Unhappy People." Even Stanley's shorter poems read like long poems. The proliferating images of "Terrace Landscapes," the profuse memory events of "San Francisco's Gone" and "San Jose Poem," and the micro-locations of "At

Andy's," as well as the "Mountains & Air" lyric sequence, all belong to the Canadian long poem being re-invented at that time by poets such as George Bowering, bp Nichol, Fred Wah, and Barry McKinnon, the latter a northern BC poet who was living, teaching, and editing Gorse Press (publisher of Stanley's *Temporarily*) in Prince George, about 200 miles east of Terrace.

•

Born in San Francisco in 1934, the elder of two brothers in an Irish-American Catholic family, Stanley became part of Jack Spicer's circle of poets and artists, participating in Spicer's "Poetry as Magic" workshop and publishing his first book of poems, *Pony Express Riders*. After Spicer's death in 1965, Stanley began to make visits to Vancouver, where UBC English professor Warren Tallman and his wife Ellen had been setting up a hospitable environment for poets associated with the San Francisco Renaissance and Donald M. Allen's 1960 anthology, *The New American Poetry*. Charles Olson, Robert Creeley, Robin Blaser, Robert Duncan, Joanne Kyger, and George Stanley had all been guests at the alternative university of the Tallman home. Stanley moved to Vancouver in 1971, working as a warehouseman and as a journalist for *The Grape*, a trade unionist offshoot of the lively pro-hippie-anti-police weekly, *The Georgia Straight*. In 1976, he was offered a job teaching English at Northwest Community College in Terrace. "San Francisco had come to an end for me in the late 1960's. Now it seemed Vancouver was coming to an end, too," he says. Moving to Terrace was like "jumping off a cliff." In the north, one has a sense of geographical vastness and cultural isolation. Stanley considered the isolation "a gift" that forged methods of composition capable of meeting the radical skepticism of postmodernist iconoclasm with a radical skepticism of his own, generated by temperament, education, compositional techniques and procedures, and the technologies of psychedelic substances. Certainly the affectionate laborious syllogistic diction of many of the poems recalls the philosophical and classical content of his high school education, which he credits for his knowledge of Virgil in Latin and Homer in Greek. The resulting prose-stanza form and its open, extensive, patient engagement with the world graces any instance with a sense of possibility:

> *I'm sitting down here in Andy's basement at Vicky's old desk*
> *on a hot Sunday in August thinking I should write about*
> *something, or rather, that I should (emphasize should) write*
> *(emphasize write) to justify my existence — my life — to*
> *myself & then having justified self, I can be with others,*
> *have a drink with Andy, e.g. without feeling self-unjustified*
> *(un-self-justified?)*

•

George Stanley has produced a powerful body of work over forty years, a poetry singular in what poet and critic Ron Silliman describes as the "ease and deftness" of its line and its "acuity of vision." Though Stanley's work is well-known in BC, where the print runs of his books sell out and his readings are packed, as well as in the States, it has received little critical attention in Canada where the canonical status one would expect of a poet of his calibre has not been forthcoming. He won the Shelley Memorial Prize from the Poetry Society of America in 2006 for a selected poems, *A Tall, Serious Girl,* published by Qua Books in the USA, placing him in the company of W.S. Merwin, Alice Notley, and Adrienne Rich among others; and in 2011 was celebrated in a 200-page special issue of *The Capilano Review*. Even so, serious academic critical attention has yet to be given to his work. Though he became a Canadian citizen in 1978 while living in Terrace, where he says he realized what it was to live in Canada, Stanley's perceived "Americanness" may yet remain an obstacle to his full acceptance into the Canadian canon. As a direct import from San Francisco who had known Jack Spicer, Charles Olson, and Robert Creeley, George Stanley would have been associated with the Black Mountain poetics then beginning to infiltrate the Canadian poetry scene, even though Stanley's major influence at that time was the post-Yeatsian Irish poet, Patrick Kavanagh, and it was work, conversation, and pub poems that occupied his oeuvre.

Another obstacle to Stanley's being recognized as a major national poet was the impact on his career of living and teaching in the hinterland. The move to Terrace coincided with the final stages of the transfer of poetic activity (conversation, dissidence, attractions) from bars, pubs, cafes, and bookstores to the university seminar room, where poet-professors such as Robert Kroetsch and Frank Davey were teaching contemporary poetry and poetics — including the work of San Francisco Renaissance and Black Mountain poets. Stanley's moving north could have been an untimely career move in an era in which a poet's strategic career moves, especially in relation to academia, began to matter. For whatever reason Stanley's work has not received the national attention it deserves, it is hoped that the publication of this volume will help to correct the imbalance.

•

The poem that opens this volume, "Icarus," is one of many about crossings, voyages, transport, and flight. Myth informs many of the poems in *Opening Day*, including a thematic concern with the Orphic myth of descent and retrieval — not of "truth" but of a generative exactitude. Since his move back to Vancouver in 1993 to take a job at Capilano College (later University), Stanley has more than half seriously promulgated the poetics of "Aboutism", his rebuttal to the excesses of the "language-centred" excesses of the poetic avant garde. Stanley's "Aboutist" methodology is apparent, though in those years unarticulated as such, in this volume, exemplified in poems as early as "Gentle Northern Summer," which concerns itself with its unfolding content: ideas, thoughts, locales, occasions, persons, and words. Later, Stanley's aboutism would be buffed up to "Aboutisme du Nord": a riposte against poetry's colonization by French theory.

Aboutism and transportation are natural companions, one enabling the other throughout *North of California St.* Stanley's first book is entitled *Pony Express Riders*; his next-to-last, *Vancouver: A Poem*, was written while riding the bus between North Vancouver and his home in Kitsilano, a journey that involves crossing Burrard Inlet on the Sea Bus. To get to and from Terrace, along with "CBC brass" and timber executives, Stanley would fly nervously on small planes, some of them bush planes. The "Mountains & Air" lyric sequence is an Aboutist text from the point of view of someone encountering a *terra incognita*. Stanley's airplane poems are almost always about mortality and fatality. Flight is a subject that creates opportunities for fear of the loss of "plain reality," of losing touch with the earth, which Stanley likens to "the truth." The sense of loss, inspired by flight, of the world, the person, the real, and the familiar, is not a backward-glancing nostalgia for a "golden" past, which we know, or are told we know, is a fiction; but rather derives from a sensed absence or emptiness in the present. In an essay about the late James Liddy, an Irish contemporary of Stanley's who taught poetry in the Milwaukee, Wisconsin, Stanley notes that Liddy's poems (much like his own, I would say) "open outward into the world, thus allowing the incarnate (opposite of virtual) object to be subject." As in Stanley's own work in this volume, "the real refuses to submit to the schema, the length of time in the line. Images come faster than they can be accommodated; the charge is to grasp the moment in its flight." In Stanley's hockey poem "The Puck," the puck is "the word" — a striking metaphor. As Stanley writes, "you can't cross the river / you can't cross the blue line / ahead of the puck":

> *The child the word the bird the butterfly the puck. They have no need of us. They keep repeating (unless the entire system of our love closes down, leaving us only these games —*

xiii

But where our care does go, where it is wanted with a
chemical hunger, is the willing, dying speaker.

In *North of California St.* are also travel poems, mostly about Ireland, where Stanley visited James Liddy, with whom he shared an affection for the poetry of Patrick Kavanagh. The poem "A Trip in Ireland" holds George Stanley and James Liddy together as poets. Ireland belongs to both of them as a vital ancestral place. Toward the end of a pub lunch in Coolgreany, Liddy has observed that "the time of men is gone" and "the ham was fine." Stanley writes, about the feeling of that moment, that he is only "one [poet] of all who are here" and that the "falling of words" composes a mutuality, an interanimation. Perhaps the feminine in this gathering, the anima of the interanimation, is death forestalled, is poetry herself:

> *One of many poets — one of all who are here — this one of*
> *all of us. No trepidation here in Ireland (look that up). No*
> *fear of the moment, the time (now) is safe in the past. Our*
> *deaths are after, not now. This moment is always (& always)*
> *reclaimed by the symbolic, by the falling of words into place*
> *(like dominoes?) — like leaves. The words carry the urgency,*
> *shoulder it, it's their own. The soul is relieved ('My burden is*
> *light'), & the body lies down, laved in the river of life, with*
> *just the sense organs protruding. Like a hippopotamus.*
>
> *'Will you have the last pint with me?' And the angel moved*
> *in & out of consciousness, ungraspable.*

The work in this volume should confirm that the author of "Veracruz," of "Berlin Wall," of "Sex at 61" and of "BC for bill bissett" is one of Canada's most talented, and, according to an enthusiastic and informed readership, one of its most accomplished poets.

xiv

1

Icarus

for Jim Herndon

In the middle of my life I found myself
on a plane from Denver to San Francisco.
Sweaty & shaking from last night's whiskey,
in aerodynamics I was losing my faith.

But the guy in the next seat took time to explain
jet flight, & he blew on a stiff piece of paper
to show how the wing worked, but it fell to the floor,
& I thought, I won't see California again;

we'll crash in the Superstition Mountains instead.
Drank Scotch, sweated more, & prayed to the engines,
while he wrote equations on a yellow pad.

They said: Weightless drop is the price of survival.
Then the plane banked, the Western horizon
steepened, & I passed the crest of the mortal.

Opening Day

for Mike Heintz

They had come back from some explosion, bomb
or quake   in the back of my head   like the beginning
of a splitting

headache, but just the beginning

& then nothing from the other side.

Giacometti hit by a truck, Montaigne
with the stone   rejoiced,

something happened in the real world

but no real world would happen to me
grew more intense   They wanted out

collective

Well, when I had to explode,
I would explode,
and there they would be

my mother's family
Emmett & Frank & Marie
alive & dancing
eating & drinking

I didn't call it a miracle. They were shades
& thru them I could see the smoking ruins
& feel the pain / I have never felt.

(& everybody had their loud opinion
on this   I thought I had to too

thought this real   which kept slipping
back
to the split second
of catastrophe

had to be kept going
by loud opinions

•

The Queen's face   face up   in Malone's white box
decorated with shamrocks
                              I danced,
drunkenly, to your Irish Country,
a jar of Guinness in my right hand

splashing / I
fell on my ass, there was

mixed applause.   Mixed with forbearance.

'We pretended we didn't know you,'
you said.   Oh, Mike, I
was pretending

from way back

•

But I mistook it.   Took the loudness for creation

not cheer. The click
of the pool balls   is more like it   the players

not smiling
unnecessarily

•

This was a necessary mistake.   To pretend it was mine
to make   or speak for   as protected by the prayers

of a hundred nuns / I careened

Larkin St. to North Beach
Potrero Hill to Hamburger Mary's
the Sunset to Haight & Cole

Always in the background were these unsmiling faces
sons   daughters   the girl who sold me ice cream

tender-faced girls, unsmiling
flat, toneless voices.   I ranted & squeaked & cried

Quit yer rhapsodizin', sez Bronley

you are not the first one to be tossed
in the waves

& Bev: You belong

to the City

not the reverse

•

Opening Day at Candlestick
up the escalator

Up the steps to the sun, & the roar

'travel poster clouds,' half of
Candlestick Point sheared off   little trees

terror
           every fist, mouth, mother
and mother-to-be   down the first base line

triumphing

Then the voice came off the crowd:

This Roman mob
grew up out of
La Belle San Francisco
just like I did

& I knew they triumphed

not over me, not over my, mine

mind

not over mind

but over darkness, iso-
lation, as the staring
of windows, the eyes of cars
& streetcars

& most of all the Victorians,
crouched in jealous rows on the hills

tall dark rooms we had stayed in
too long

now out in the sun!

•

Darkness out of which we all had come

& to which we'd go back, if need be.

& back from which we'd come again, if needed.

San Francisco's Gone

for Gerald, much love

and in memory of
Edward Dermott 'Ned' Doyle
who taught me poetry
and gave me reasons to travel
north of California St.

1

For a fraction of a second behind tired eyes
image of SF waterfront circa 1950
from deck of SP ferry
                         emerging from beneath
double-deck Bay Bridge; splayed piers flank
Arthur Paige Brown's Ferry Building,
'20s skyscrapers, Russ & the phone company,
& the nozzle atop Telegraph Hill, in scale
with the human houses, high-ceilinged neighborhoods,
ascending steep slopes of bluebrown Twin Peaks.

All night drinking on the train
from Stockton: USF football game,
Dons beat COP 56-7 (?)
— the train must have been shunted over Western Pacific
tracks — I think we passed through Tracy — or held on
sidings, to take all night to get from Stockton to Oakland
(80 miles?)

I started drinking beer that summer, with Tom Gallagher,
Bert Schaefer, and Neil Battaglia, in Tom's car, parked
somewhere out in the Sunset with the lights out, a
weekday night, cold quarts of Burgie or Regal Pale in
paper bags.

In June I'd graduated from SI, walked up the center aisle of St. Ignatius twice — once for the Martin Latin medal and once for the scholarship to USF — then last, in alphabetical order, to accept the ribbon-tied scroll from the priest sitting in a carved armchair below the altar (my rival, LaForest 'Frosty' Phillips, beat me though; he went up for three prizes)

I was a sissy in high school, & got picked on a lot, & so, started hanging out with these older guys, Tom, Bert, and Neil (whom I'd impressed with my wits, I could make them laugh), I'd met working as a page after school at the Main Library (McAllister & Larkin, architect George Kelham, 1917(?)), & drinking beer (so maybe it was earlier than that summer)

Drank vodka (in a bag) for the first time at a college 'smoker' & woke up the next morning in the back seat of somebody's convertible, splattered with the necessary dried vomit, the car being parked not on any street but askew in the parking lot at the center of campus, many students at 10 o'clock class break peeking in the window

& became a football fan. That year the Dons went undefeated, so, traveled on the chartered fans' train to Stockton to see them whomp COP. Next Monday USF was ranked 10th in the UPI coaches' poll. 1951, Ollie Matson's year.

San Francisco, as it looked then.

2

Her first day at the office
all lunch hour she walked around the block
too shy to go in a restaurant

One of several times I visited my Aunt Catherine, my mother's younger sister, a nun in her seventies, at the convent in San Jose, she told this story. We were sitting in the sunny visitors' parlor, on spotless upholstered furniture, that had been my mother's.

If she went to work at 17, that would have been 1921 or -2. I imagine the building as Kelham's Standard Oil of California headquarters at Bush & Sansome (that went up in '21). After her dad lost his coal & wood yard in Daly City (gas now cheap enough for cooking), she had to go to work. Big corporations were hiring women for office work — SP, Standard Oil, PG&E (that sold the gas). Catherine would have been 13.

California corporations put up neo-Gothic skyscrapers (25 stories, tops) on landfill placed in the '70s over the wrecks of sailing ships (the original waterfront was just east of Montgomery)

I imagine the block she walked around as Bush Montgomery Pine Sansome, every building new or under construction, bare steel & the flash & sputter of oxy-welding, excavations, wagons, horses, men: a boom built on fire insurance proceeds (five Eastern companies bankrupted) & loans from the new Bank of America (backed by grain & fruit receipts)

Jack had come out from Cork in the '90s. (His cousins in Menlo Park who had emigrated earlier thought of Jack (and Mamie, whose father Michael was a day laborer) as 'Irish', but considered themselves 'Californians' (this is also Catherine's memory).) When he lost his business he went to work for C&H Sugar, the Hawaiian growers' refinery in Crockett. Boarded, came home weekends & Christmas. The gold 25-year pin with diamond chip, which

11

he received on retirement (and which was sent to me after
Catherine's death, in 1985, by the Sisters) reads: *J. Hennessy
4–16–41.*

25 years a farm boy in West Cork, 25 or so an Irish-
Californian worker, then merchant, then at 50 a sugar
worker. Mamie and the four children moved back
downtown, to a flat in an alley off 15th & Church. Marie
would have taken the 'J', or one of the Market cars, to
work. Mamie (or Mary, as she wrote on job applications)
went to work for the SP, when Catherine and Francis were
older.

*For it was Mary, Mary
long before the fashion came*

Marie, a French name, why? A cachet
of elegance, before the Fire?

*Though with propriety, society
would say Ma–rie*

And the shyness, of the Catholic girl,
near country girl, grew up on a kind of farm
next to a coal & wood yard

Brown hair, fair skin, freckled.
Hazel eyes. *Petite*, five-one.

Learned her Palmer hand
at Mission Dolores, typing
at the office. Early as I can remember,

the grocery list with one or two items
neatly crossed out. She could balance her checkbook.

12

3

The first-born, her brother Emmett,
graduate of Sacred Heart, attending
night law school at St. Ignatius, working days
on the front desk at the St. Francis: their hope.

Imagine a weekend excursion to Santa Cruz.
The SP train leaves from 3rd & Townsend.
Emmett, his sister Marie, his girl friend Regina,
his friend George Stanley from the hotel.
Cousin Mary gets on at Menlo. They take

a couple of cabins in a tourist court
near the beach. Do they bring
blankets from the City or borrow the ones in the cabin
to spread on the sand? The striped
beach umbrella goes up, the girls in one-piece
suits (& caps if they go in), the men
in baggy trunks run in the surf, their feet
slap the wet sand, they bat
the beach ball. Big green waves
off Monterey Bay break.

In the evening
they walk the boardwalk, or 'invest'
a dime in the player piano with seven
percussion instruments banging in the Casino.
Throw the baseball, knock over the milk bottles.
The booth lights glance in the soft waves
of the girls' hair.

& back at the cabin play swing records
on the wind-up Victrola (I guess),
& later in the decade
mix orange blossoms: canned juice

& bathtub gin. Young, happy
white collar workers

Happy to return to the City

    4

George (there was a photograph, part of his face in
    slanting shadow, the mouth obscure)
was in the Navy,

was out in the Atlantic once, on a destroyer but not far,
    nowhere near the U-boats
(the war — for improvement — like the Panama Canal)

At Pelham Bay Naval Station, New York, he had the 'flu.
Discharged in '19, sailed for home, & to return

to his widowed father, George Albert Stanley, civil
    engineer
and Grand Secretary of the Young Men's Institute (the
    Catholic 'Y'), club & baths at 50 Oak St.,

living in an apartment on Turk, or Octavia . . . check the
    city directory.

The ex-sailor was George *Anthony* Stanley,
the friar patron of lost belongings exchanged
for the Prince Consort. And that was his mother,
Molly McCormick's, gift.

Did Marie tell me he wrote poetry? Or that, en route, he
    stayed, several days, a sojourn
(or was it just a shore visit, a few hours?)
in Havana, Cuba, & thought of not
coming back, but going on to Brazil?

14

because that's where I imagine him, a serious — a *dreamy*,
dark, narrow-headed boy, with stiff black hair. I see him
at a table (marble top) in a sidewalk cafe, or walking the
Malecón into a summer wind, but can't imagine how he
imagined

that break, what image, song, or deeper will
called him —
but instead returned

to the Grand Secretary, who lives at the William Taylor
Hotel on McAllister, & takes all his meals out now,
accompanied by his boy,

and a job on the front desk at the St. Francis.

Emmett invites him up to his mother's place, at 11 Carl.
In the front room Ma plays the upright, a
vigorous bass, bright treble, plinking
above high C, rippling streams.

Then the girls gather round chorusing,
'Come, Josephine, In My Flying Machine'

& the men, in good clothes, seated
on Mamie's mahogany furniture, served
cake & claret.

     5

They were good houses, built by small contractors
working out of sheds in alleys, mixing concrete & pouring
foundations, blueprints on site. On the side streets —

Clayton, Shrader — wider types of Queen Anne Victorian
— big, gabled attics, broad sidewalks for play. On Carl

(the arterial, later the car-line) older, narrower styles, flat
roofs. The Haight

is forty years or so old, in '33. Sunny Jim had been Mayor,
now Governor. You repainted your house every five years,
you & your brother-in-law. Borrow the ladder. With a hoist
you could tar your own roof.

Now down the north side of Haight of a Spring morning
comes Mrs. Murphy, a fat (not stout) French (Franco-
American?) lady, in black (like the other morning
shoppers) — black straw hat, black purse, & in the purse
the worn leather change purse; from the Superba, crossing
at Cole, in front of the stopped Haight cars, wagons
& trucks, to Romey's, to get canteloupe or celery 3¢
cheaper. Her new downstairs tenant, Marie Stanley, often
accompanies her, but not today, she ran up Carl to her
mother's place, number 11.

The front parlor of Ma's upstairs flat (Marie walks down
the hall) is silent, as is the back dining room. Jack is in
Crockett. Marie sits at the kitchen table. Ma comes up the
back stairs with marigolds, picked from slat-bordered beds
in the backyard. Pokes the fire in the grate, moves some
stewing apples away from the heat, pours coffee. She sits
down across from Marie, who tells her hesitant secrets.

Sunlight sparkles in the high windows; outside, clothes on
the line wave, trees in other yards. The bride & the bride's
mother talk, of the new husband and the old one, the one
away, the father. The things to be done for the men who
come home.

(When I saw the bride's face at Carew & English
not looking upward from the satin,

16

I saw by the line of her jaw it was my grandmother's,
previously concealed by amiable laughter)

   6

& George went to the PG&E for a year —
on the iron monster, through the new Sunset Tunnel —

then the Hall, with its green-patina'd dome
   (was it gilt in '15?), Arthur Brown, Jr.'s
couchant-sphinx headquarters, with wings for legs
   (when whizbangs flew & mustard gas crept
at Ypres), colonnaded tribute to Sunny Jim Rolph's
   honest administration, and symbol
of the new City risen from the ashes, after

years of graft, trials of the Board of Supervisors,
Boss Ruef's creatures, interrupted by the Fire, was to be
the major effect in Daniel Burnham's 'City Beautiful' plan,
   if hungry businessmen had not
sunk that dream (hardly vision), gone back to making
   money on the
old plat, stacking bricks the morning after
the Fire
       (and well they did, can you imagine the City's hills
draped in landscaped avenues, like ramps on the
   contours?)

The Fire that George remembers (he was eight, walked
   with his father to the north/south ridge of the City,
Laurel Hill cemetery (they were living somewhere out out
on Turk), walked with thousands up to the Park, there
   they turned around, looked east.
On that April day, winds blew. Sky was red. 50,000 people
   stood & watched

the red sky, & then the red & black sky, & heard all day &
    all night, the roar
of the flames, & the falling of buildings.

& on the weekend, smart guys neatly stacked the bricks
(but who could, Bean* says somewhere, tell the lessees
    from the looters?)

        7

Late afternoon. Fog comes, in gusts, streamers,
then a damp wall over the Park. The custard-white
spires of St. Ignatius shine bright above. Like bishops.

Sand is still blowing in the Sunset, houses
hammered in the sand dunes, boys climging in the
    unbuilt.

    8. UNDER THE DOME

A 12' oak-paneled office, upper walls off-white.
Black tabulating & card-sorting machines. The boy sits
at an unused desk, randomly fingering the keys
of a comptometer. The man turns

from the women in black smocks with white
lace collars (who turn too), a white card
in a black wood frame, held out,
a word in black caps, glassed:

> ### THINK
>   IBM

* Walton Bean, California historian.

18

Then down the marble corridor
of the north wing to a second office.
Women looked up from their typing,
they worked for him, as he worked
for Mr. Brooks, & Tom Brooks worked for Mayor Rossi.
    Part of the dome is seen,
chalk-green, in a window above him.

FDR was President, Pius XII Pope, Joe Louis
heavyweight champion. We were winning the war,
a sure thing, but he, though complacent
as any Democrat, disliked the routine.
He knew the City was built on sand and an
underground river, that they pumped
water out of the Opera House basement 24 hrs. a day.

What was in front of
my face when he held out
that card in its black frame
but his body, white shirt, Paisley tie
hanging, belt & buckle. (The card lay
in the top drawer of the highboy years, under socks.)

When he threw me in the ocean
I can't even remember yelling,
only running back up the sand
to the umbrella, remains of picnic lunch.
Ocean Beach. (The sand was dirtier now,
there were things in it. Bottle caps.)

In his office he tried to show the boy
the trustworthiness of the City, souls
shaped by official duties.
He couldn't believe it.
So we went back to water.

In the clammy indoor pool
of the YMI, the boy
willed his body to sink, would not
be buoyant.

        Of what
importance is it except to do
justice to the pain of his want,
his lack, holding out a gift that was not
his to give, his version of manhood, boyhood.
He was not a giver. He was a poet,
   a sailor,

manqué. The boy rejected
the mirage projected
from some beyond
& bounced off Ireland.

We stood naked in the shower room
& his will backfired on his eye,
his secret passion stole the boy away
on waves of adventure, & in that moment,
   his lostness
was the true gift.

   9

Once, on the streetcar, the 'L', going downtown,
a sunny Saturday, maybe the fall of '47,
him 48, me 13, heads bent, an intense
conversation, in the dark, varnished seats
at the back of the car. It had begun

even before we sat down, taking transfers
from the conductor (were we going
to the ball game?) I could tell

he wanted out, that he looked toward San Diego
(we had spent a couple of weeks there, that summer)

as he had to Brazil. There were breezes & shadows,
the iron monster rolled smoothly along Market
from Castro to Sanchez. He had a grey hat on
with the snap brim turned up
all around. We wore thin McGregor jackets,
grey or beige. We were almost friends.

He told me what it meant to be
George Stanley, with only wit as a plea.
He tried to pass on to me
the name, Anthony, his mother had found
to replace the alien Albert. He wanted me

to be Tony, it fit the land, he said, like Mission
architecture, women liked it. I could not
take that talisman, happiness, from him.
Loyally I chose to continue his fuckup.

10

Ten years later he comes home on the 'L',
the pink *Call-Bulletin* folded under his arm,
takes off his hat, in the kitchen
lifts his glass of Roma port to her, tells her
(again) how he hates the place,
the Hall. The leisurely civil service manner
adopted by Blacks or Samoans seems to him
misconduct.

11. ISLANDS

All the islands swam across the Atlantic
and became parishes in New York
JAMES LIDDY

But James, some of them must have swum
further, by Panama portage come to a Golden Gate,
a Catholic country whose cathedral debt was paid
by transcontinental train time ('69).

                               Shanty Irish
south o' the slot, & lace curtain Irish
sticking flowers in vases to place on tables
even when there was nobody dead.

                                  Tobins
of the Hibernia sucked deposits to the
heights (like, Ashbury?), & lent them out
past the panic of '73 when even Ralston
(of the Bank of California, he who had planted
eucalyptus seeds in the Panhandle) jumped in the Bay;

small factories, one or two storey buildings,
iron workers, brass founders, flour millers,
stiching bags to fill, wagons to carry
    cross town,
living in flats over stores, yet building,
out Mission & Howard & Folsom (where Mission makes
the big bend towards Spain), *palaces* . . .

'copies of fragments of palaces . . . thin, wooden, box-
    like structures with bay windows,' thus Arthur Paige
    Brown's scorn for the people's
mansions, Victorians he saw first in the '80s,

22

brown-wallpapered, tintype-laden, gas-lit,
that packed the 11th ward, & pushed out

toward Daly City, farms.

Small families. Not because of safes
but diphtheria. To their priceless
children, nuns spoke
blandly of Hell, at the bottom of space,
with its tortures,
                    & even in the public
schools, teachers said, 'absolution,'
faced down nativist rage.

The islands: St. Joseph's, St. Rose's, St. Peter's.
St. John the Baptist, on Eddy. St. Agnes
(of the Haight). St. Anne of the Sunset.

12. THE WHITE CLIFFS OF DOELGER

Henry J., developer, when land was free
& work was cheap (& the 17 car 5 cents)
financed and oversaw the building of
good houses in long, north-south blocks

on the Parkside slope. Retained damp sand
by concrete wall, water pipes
the City put in, big creosoted redwood poles,
crossarm'd, upheld the wires (as they still do).

Each bungalow, stucco'd, painted white (a few
pink, yellow, green — the colors of frosted cakes)
looked down blacktop streets with white lines

to the Pacific. And the ocean breathed its condensation
  back

high as Twin Peaks over my head
all spring & early summer, morning's womb.

13

From the earliest she dwelt in Heaven, its brown, sloping
   hills
that California bruited as an afterlife
for suffering Ireland. Gossoons,
unmarried at 40, made their way here,
stepped stiffly from the train at Oakland Pier,
bachelor uncles needing to be cooked for.

These were the duties of the daughters, to turn
the profusion of Paradise into family meals.
The gas range saved her labor but demanded
by its white enamel hauteur more devotion
(& kneeling polishing Mondrian linoleum)
than her mother's wood floors & coal hod
& lump coal in dusty bags leaning by the pantry.

Then needed a green car to drive her mother
to doctors. The young men of the good time still wearing
collar & tie toed it to the Park from the rest home run by
'that woman' to whom she wrote checks.

She was on *some other work*, her clothing,
serviceable coats, hats with perfunctory veil,
showed it: determination & later hair color.
She wore flowers like they were ornaments.

In the bath she would wash my hair, then rub it dry,
brisk, detached. The phone would ring during dinner.

And kept all the accounts. Angel of mercy
arriving on time, Hayward or Hayes St.

24

Later schoolchildren
knew her reliability, her love.

In the hospital, on Darvon, she patted her thigh
where the cancer grew & said, 'My friend.'

14

After her death, George & George & Gerald
walking up Taraval from the Riviera Restaurant
(not North Beach of the '50s, but credible Italian food,
water & a basket of bread on the table before ordering),

Dad walked away into the shade of a building
to pee. So there we were, like we didn't need
facilities. No longer separate in time, but in fact
friends, boys, three sons of a dead saint.

15. HER DREAM

In the Sunset, in the '50s, her soul breathes easy.
She walks to the retail, noting with approval
disappearance of vacant lots, sand & iceplant,
houses & stores going up, even without lawns,
flush with the sidewalk; & from her back window sees
terraced houses, white blocks,
covering up the dunes, leaving only
a strip of beach: families moving
in, taming finally this almost empty
Spanish shore, home to seagulls, a sense
of reward for rightness.

                    Now there's happiness,
a living room furnished from the Emporium,
rose brocade drapes, gold sofa & chairs,
tables, & friends make up a club, a parish

salary-rich, a new church, bell
tower & baldacchino (fixed canopy over the altar)
rises from the striped parking lot
(Archbishop Mitty charged the going rate on the loan).

The City is built now, it stays poised
here for a moment, respectable,
inviting speculation, till a generation
dies or moves down the Peninsula.

Marie has the club over
after Christmas midnight mass.

A police lieutenant, the vice-president
of Cal-Pak, big men in blue suits,
gripping highballs, stand in her living room
(& George stands among them, in white shirt & tie, but
    not quite
of them, something odd about him, McGinty, the VP, has
    said,
not unkindly, mind somewhere else.

                                        Marie bustles
among the men & their wives, with hors d'oeuvres
The blue & silver balls gleam on the artificial tree
& Crosby sings on the hi-fi, 'Adeste . . .'

After they leave something takes her back.
A holy card in her missal. Her thoughts go back
to the Mission, she sees again
the crowded streets, where it all went on
in flesh and blood. Streetcars clanged,
priests hurried past, to the sick,
her aunts dressed in black for shopping,
butcher on 16th St. with the sawdust
& pink butcher paper — living world —

26

& all seemed to know it was one —
bread meat fur flowers —
moves her heart, not Paradise
but plain reality lost.

Illusion, I want to tell her.
Like the Milky Way, the galaxy seen
through its longest dimension, packed with stars.

I wanted to tell her the stars walk alone.

Time packs truths closer, events flock on hills of
   knowledge
(& she nods & smiles, dreaming alone)

Her truth now wakes in my mind
& where there was bleakness or a gash in meaning

(George & George & Gerald sat in the coffee shop
on Polk St., a block down from the hospital,
commenting lamely on the service, the waitress, even
half-heartedly joking, for each other, then in silence
turned back to her again, her worn, sweet face — she
loved — it doesn't matter who

We can part, Marie & I,
if we can each remember
a mother whose eyes showed care,
the home look

Sometimes, a heart waits
unable to answer, or do more than
look from the window,
fondly, unseen

Marie, who bore me.

16. VERACRUZ

In Veracruz, city of breezes & sailors & loud birds,
an old man, I walked the Malecón by the sea,

and I thought of my father, who when a young man
had walked the Malecón in Havana, dreaming of Brazil,

and I wished he had gone to Brazil
& learned magic,

and I wished my father had come back to San Francisco
armed with Brazilian magic, & that he had married
not my mother, but her brother, whom he truly loved.

I wish my father had, like Tiresias, changed himself into a
    woman,
& that he had been impregnated by my uncle, & given
    birth to me as a girl.

I wish that I had grown up in San Francisco as a girl,
a tall, serious girl,

& that eventually I had come to Veracruz,
& walking on the Malecón, I had met a sailor,
a Mexican sailor or a sailor from some other country —
    maybe a Brazilian sailor,
& that he had married me, & I had become pregnant by
    him,
so that I could give birth at last to my son — the boy I love.

San Jose Poem

for Catherine Hennessy
(Sister Maureen) (1908–1985)

Starting in April, sadness
carried forward from Catherine's death
which I have not mourned, in April,
in April sadness

how the city of San Jose stands in my mind,
the B of A with its bell-less tower,
hot 5 p.m., walking east on Santa Clara
cross Market and First

preserved façades,
south between Second and Third
sun on car roofs, blocks
razed to keep Mexicans from crossing
(some stores left hang
banners in Vietnamese)

South of Keyes
were orchards

•

       Sunday afternoons
we drove to orchards

a grey DeSoto
or Dodge sedan, moving slowly down
gravel roads
quarter-sections of trees
geometrically spaced,
watered

the grey Coast hills
beyond

Visitors, we parked
in front of a small barn,
were allowed to walk in among the trees,
reached into our hands & mouths
Santa Clara plums, a sweet
green fig, ripe apricots.
Our friends gave us balsa cartons
to take fruit back to the City.

·

Catherine came
to San Jose as Superior
of the convent, her last assignment.
12 years she had been Superior of the Order.

At her funeral mass Gerald said
(in his homily) she was not one of the foolish virgins
nor would she have been one of the 'sensible' virgins
either, refusing oil to her foolish sisters,
telling them to go downtown to buy some

She would have been in the Lord's house already
placing a glass of gingerale and a cookie
in the room of each one arriving home late

as she came to the side door
of the Hayes St. convent in San Francisco
with wax-paper sandwiches
of cabbage & mashed potato
for men who lined up
in the Depression.

•

Catherine entered the Sisters
of the Holy Family in 1930.
The order, since 1872,
patronized by Irish banks, established
day homes, for children of
poor: in San Jose,
cannery workers.

                    The fruit
left by train. The trees
sucked the water out of the ground
& it left as fruit. Water in a well
(Santa Clara & Delmas)
150 ft. (1950).

The sisters lived in underheated
California baroque luxury (mahogany paneling).

Sr. Thomasine held me as a child.

Last year, St. Daniel, her sister, served
shrimp salads, steaks, rolls, ice cream & coffee
to Catherine & me
in the Superior's dining room.

These people are still alive
& live on St. Elizabeth's Drive
in San Jose (& they are dead & live in this poem
with the often repetitive movements of the dead,
drawing in a skirt, just so, as to be remembered
in rooms filled with spring sunlight
& my mother's spotless furniture.

•

Leaving the convent, dazed, dazzled
by goodness I'd go back to the Holiday Inn
generously contemptuous of the ones who ate avocado
salads in the Hawaiian coffee shop or played
video games in the black alcove

& on leaving the Inn
walk up Almaden
past the offshore banks
(the orchards burnt & dozed
when electronics came)

think of recent Santa Clara grads
hoping to retain the software concession,
steal the yup trade from Mountain View, fill the new
Civic Center with suits, music, beds of flowers, &
    sprinklers!

•

In the old day homes
these virgins were my mothers.
I was treated
as poor.

On the polished hardwood floor
rolling in play pants. In black habit
& stiff white coif
Thomasine bends to offer

penuché on a glass plate. Downstairs,
admitted to the working areas, the stone-floored kitchen,
Sr. Malachy supervising,
two Spanish women baking,

door open on a walled garden,
a red or yellow watering can, geraniums,
tall bending stalks of snapdragon.

Catherine remembers me asking questions.
'Is it all right?' 'No.' (My mother's voice.)
'It it all wrong?' Nuns smiling. One eternal
moment the content of the other, as we sit,
talking.

Paradise Shelter

for Russell FitzGerald (1932–1978)

1

Children's lives
are
fragmentary

They don't know
what's
going on

Episodic,
Robert Duncan
said.

In which rooms
have I seen
paradise

tottered
toward it
& been distracted

in which lives
assaulted
Eden.

Incomprehensible
languages
separate

us,
we grapple
w/ fragments

of reason
shattered
mind.

2

Did vacant lots
or bare squares,
bourgeois parks

breathe back our words?
All irregular
perspectives

beckoned
(mouthwateringly)
& took the heat off us

& we strolled
becomingly for our time
imparting the requisite

quantum of gladness,
a feather
in the balance.

3

Did some now-hidden
goddess nurse
our freshly-shaved
philosophy?

Wit fueled by anguish
& contempt
but flowering into
story yet

Thought public as all Hell
but Art,
the way (Der Weg —
Olson) lost

The method hidden
from ourselves
Hermetic
not by choice

1961,
New York.
Paradise
a joke.

Where Hell is
people live
Your eyes & mine
decided that

& then later in Hell
swallowed the New
like a corrosive chemical
Stupid to blame culture . . .

4

In desolate
location
innumerable

projection-beam
universes
flash

Who dare dream
of happiness
They don't know

what's going on
what dreams
underlie

every step
even those
that stumble

The dreams of the blind
the numb dreams
of the one

whose worship
has been found
wanting.

5

The Emerald City
shining over
the burnt-out slums
of North Philadelphia.

Like reality,
the approaching
PTC streetcar also wobbles
on its tracks . . .

A splendid mockery
or a mocking splendor

The altarpieces you fashioned,
Michelangelo-like, in your mind

the world that while it loved you
gave its dreamlike substance
to be modeled
by your vision

& the lapsed, gutted churches
where even
the name
cannot be found.

6

& the body
which we all are
(like M:
came by to tell me

the goats
cd be sitting in our chairs
& us outside
trying to make a meal out of dandelions

7

You perhaps
of all of us
did not desire
to dominate.

Armando said,
he asked me up
to his room

to draw me
   & he drew me!

Eyes
at rest
the pencil
moving,

no 'privileged observer'
in that world,
this world,
or quest

imagined
unshackled
unselfish
love.

Did not
'condescend'
to illustration,
   no auteur he,
     'separate reality'

monger, or hiero-
phant.

A gawky 28-year-old Pennsylvanian.
Antagonist
of the game.

'They're furious
that a six-foot Irishman
like me is queer.
You, they expect it of.'

•

Heroes
in your life,
men
pursued by demons,
                    Spicer

named you Billy.
It was a ring of words
It rang through all the places
outside the words.

        •

The dark face
found its crown
(The body grew fatter.)
They steady look became

a long, limp gaze
on man
& woman.

Parsifal, Percival.

    8

Whatever this place is
that we will not admit
to each other we have discovered
is all there is.

Each unapproachable & fiery self
physically & symbolically
involutional.
Hiya Buddy,

40

sighted across blocks,
universes passed us
like streetcars.
We clamber

on the
outside — parasites,
we can't make contact
through our life-support systems.

A birthday candle,
a light, a shadow
or something you saw
in the air around you,

a being seeing back.

Wordless acquaintance
in search of procedure
each act of
paradise shelter.

Raft

On the raft, floating down
whatever flows, Huck & Jim
close at the center,
one facing upstream, trying not to remember,
feels the pressure
of the other's shoulders, facing down

remembering
boardinghouses, communes, bars,
working in offices & mills,
weddings & funerals & wakes

sitting smoking behind a barn
(or was that a story?)
sitting in the bleachers at ball games,
riding in cars, once over a bumpy field
in Gordon's Buick

sex . . .
a lobster dinner . . .

I thought I knew those places.
They were the world, each one,
mountains beyond mountains, kingdoms,
wisdom & shining gold, territory,
& there was a mother, a lover, a future.

Now this raft goes faster & faster
& I hold in my mind a map
that is the map of the world

& at my back my other
watches the islands come swooping
past, & feels my back
warm against his, his precious one.

Mozart & Cold Cuts

(Flight 513, Vancouver–
San Francisco, 1 June 1990

Do you think
each day
is one less?

Does the sunlight
include a ray
of its absence?

Flying
to once 'home'
(Mozart & cold cuts)

Curved cabin,
blue ocean,
surf spatter,
brown hills —
reality
never answers.

San Francisco's
there —
cool, timeless,
like it was
before nostalgia.

Faint memory
of flushed boy-face
in 1950.
Running for judge.

Mary, born
1906, says,
'When I die'.
Bowl of pink pansies.

Orators:
on streetcorner, 'George
Herbert Bush . . .',
on traffic island,
'Homosexuals . . .',
on steps of Sproul Hall,
'If I had
30,000 . . .'

Hard, the men
with blankets
& shopping carts.

In Jess's painting
Time Becomes Part of the Picture
in the form of a fly.

Blake's fly
is a man
believing.

Here, in this blue
air, do you fear?

Here,
in this blue air,
do you fear?

Under the bay,
the train

speeding in the tube
rests on mud.

Would you give
the black man
(& the woman following
pushing the cart)
3 dollars & 20 cents
for bacon & eggs?

Why cry
for Matthew Broderick
in *Glory*
and not for them?

Easter Sunday '75

Easter Sunday I take a stroll —
no, can't call it that, just a walk,
given the shade cast by the black
towers on Mayor Phillips' Granville Mall.

Next down to Victory Square.
Sunny, but there's no one there.
No pub or shop open —
Proddies all home mopin'

Back up to Pender Aud —
a mass meeting has been called
to oppose racism in suburban Surrey
Mayor Vander Zalm says don't you worry

if boyish thugs smash middle-class Sikhs' windows.
Surrey police say, you catch the guy, turn him over.
'Are you crazy?' an elegant, turbaned speaker wants to
    know.
'Do they think we would hand him over — like a flower?
No, we'll do it to him.'

Hardial Bains says there's lots of food
I say to Augie I hope it's good.
It is: boxes of hot parathas
with a bright red sauce like goes on tacos.
Jamie's mouth starts to smoke,
he says, 'Hey, where'd you get that Coke?'

Us guys trapped alive in it
don't dare distrust it for a minute
(I mean the flaming cosmos) or
the provenance of any unit.

47

Home I get stoned & drink beer with Dick
& listen to '50s rock on C-FUN
noticing how the effect of dope
is to amplify nuance, diminish vision.

Down in the Flats

Down in the flats where False Creek used to be
Vancouver reminds me of Chicago.
They aren't real stop signs, Augie says,
banging over the sidings. All
used cars take the shocks of reality,
bringing down their value.

Down in the flats where False Creek used to be
a stripper dances to flirty blues
or reasonable facsimile.
The never-thwarted moon of booze
blots out the *Vancouver Sun*. All cars
on the sidings of hope are tagged
waiting to have their seals undone.

Down in the flats where False Creek used to be
aunts & grandmothers troop through Woodward's
seeking the seals of approval.
A trucker explains the metric system,
his buddy is more interested in a novel.
Glancers at walk signals hustle
past late S.E. Asian news.

Down in the flats where False Creek used to be
strippers and grandmothers know their unity.
Truckers turning right into Pender
wink at the moon. Yet the hotels sag,
sick with the blues, and regretfully,
we can't get these seals undone.

Vancouver in April

It's pretty shitty
living in a Protestant city
& my heart too bleak for self-pity

I sit in the Cecil
surrounded by a passel
of loudmouth'd assholes

I swill beer
to still my fear
of the coming year

& there are mornings when I wake up
so riddled with psychic breakup
I can hardly hold on to my coffee cup.

I lived here three months
in a house where I never once
heard anyone say please or thanks.

Not the best indoor weather
for getting your head together
but it's a personal matter.

I walked in the rain when I felt more free
(the rain's great on UIC)
soft Vancouver rain used to console me.

But then I got a job — stripping trucks
for CP Transport. 500 bucks
a month I make, but the job sucks

& the rain gets in my knee
where some cartilage gave way
& I'd rather it were sunny, every day.

I walk to work along Hastings
where every white face seems
skewed by chronic grimacing

& the natives' smashed smiles
pitiful doglike denial
of unadmittable exile.

On Granville Mall trios of thugs
stoned on beer & soft drugs
protrude their blond, bland mugs

(The guys I work with seem all right
in the grimy lunchroom every night
under icetray fluorescent light

we scan the *Province*, don't talk much,
about the fucking foreman bitch
but on personal matters rarely touch.)

Soon will return our German August
& the sullen sons of the upper crust
their bready bodies will loll & toast

At Kits Beach & English Bay
Vancouver resounds through the long hot day
with the intense silence of solitary play

Old men sit with their single glasses
of beer, 'neath murals of buxom lasses
in the vast pub, till the evening passes

after Patrick Kavanagh

Donatello's David

1

Donatello's David
drives a CP Transport truck,
puts in two hours on the dock,
punches out at 7 o'clock.

A surly slender flower
whose petals stand up straight,
he is not noticed by the men
pulled along by the freight.

They go into the nightly jumble
on paths where the forklifts hurtle
Skids of goods are ready to topple
& the dollies turn in a circle.

2

Krishna came into my trailer,
silent as a thug,
hoisted on his shoulder snug,
a Minneapolis afghan rug.

He wonders if his future,
like the rug, is second-rate.
I did not mention it to the men
pulled along by the freight.

They go into the nightly jumble
on paths where the forklifts hurtle
Skids of goods are ready to topple
& the dollies turn in a circle.

3

Kneeling on the concrete
like the Emperor in the snow,
white-haired Abie's hammerblow
will make the busted dolly go.

The steel pin he straightens
as his body bends to Fate
past the ken of union men
pulled along by the freight.

They go into the nightly jumble
on paths where the forklifts hurtle
Skids of goods are ready to topple
& the dollies turn in a circle.

4

Easter eggs for Edmonton,
engine blocks for Trail.
Fashions off the Granville Mall
go back to shops in Montreal.

And slowly o'er the viaduct
the moon is rising late.
She sees me on the loading dock
pulled along by the freight.

I go into the nightly jumble
on paths where the forklifts hurtle
Skids of goods are ready to topple
& the dollies turn in a circle.

5

Homeward is our vision
or haplessly we work,
& it's like a prayer, I know
it's like a prayer, I know
it's like a prayer, I know,
each time we say the word fuck.

Each time we say the word fuck,
we go into the nightly jumble
on paths where the forklifts hurtle
Skids of goods are ready to topple
& the dollies turn in a circle.

'Chateau Sleaze'

for Richard

That winged chariot behind our ears
flashing on the prisms of the air
like the Aurora Borealis, cheers
no one; so we sit each in his chair

contemplating verity. The charioteer
drives his team through our silences
& waving his spectral spear,
punctuates our careful confidences.

We never got a proper curtain for
that window, did we? Broke since January.
Your charioteer is just a character
from literature, an advert for a mortuary.

Quiet your ancient fears, let chains of grace
crisscross the faded dining room like lace.

The Set

Remembering how it felt
working on the *Grape*
in '72, doing layout
in a gray former grocery
on Powell — we'd take a break
at suppertime & head for the pub,
knock back six or eight draft,
a package or two of chips,
maybe a pickled sausage,
& tell the waiter,
'Take one for yourself.'

We were a part of history
in our mental spotlight, drinking beer
with trade unionists from the '30s
in that battered pub (soon to be closed,
renovated & turned into a fern bar).
They told us tales
of struggles of the past.

We'd troop back, half-lit
through snowy darkness or summer shadow
to that gray, dingy, dimly-lit
former grocery, to finish our layout.
There was never enough liner
or blades for the X-Acto knives & the
typeset 'corrections' always came late
from the *Peak* & had to be pasted
in by hand, but the beer in our heads
kept us going past midnight — also the link
with the old union guys — with the dirty '30s —
we were for real — & we were dirty.

Do you miss all that? Do you miss the dirty '70s?
That sense there was a world & meaning
outside your mind? Tho skeptic Ed Dorn
said 'the set', you could account
not just for the world but for nature itself:
the trees that leafed in the spring on Powell St.,
the stars — for you thought,
why would there be stars if there were
no world for them to shine on?

& by the third or fourth draft
your hangover would lift
& there'd be the sacred streets, in long
purple & orange stripes of sunset
to the eternal horizon,

& you called yourself a cadre,
a little yeast cell, making
tiny, correct changes in people's
consciousness, getting the paper out
on the streets. Miss all that?

I shot up to Rupert for no reason
like a steel ball in a Bally machine,
banging around the pink bumpers,
racking up points for god knows who or what.

I came almost to a stop, poised at the entrance
to one of those long, gently raked, steel alleys
you can roll down for years, decades, & still
be far from the flippers. Then I missed the world,
the beery romance of politics,
(the whiskey romance of poetry),
the set.

The Berlin Wall

Why, now that it's breached, broken, does it cause
such consternation in me?

                                        CBC brings me
the cries of happy youth, the singing, people
climbing up on the now meaningless Wall,
drinking champagne —

                                        I see myself
eighteen months ago at Checkpoint Charlie,
hurrying across the street to avoid
the grisly American museum —

                                        In the narrow corridor,
slipped my Canadian passport under glass to the
    unsmiling
visor-capped uniformed young official — he inserts a visa,
passes it back — a loud buzzer sounds, a door swings open
into the next holding-pen — exchange West marks for
    East marks,
another buzzer, another door — a block or so of speed
    bumps &
barriers to control cars —

                                        then on Friedrichstrasse I stand,
an official, legal visitor to the Deutsche Demokratische
    Republik,
approved museum-goer, café patron, *flâneur* . . .

The past is a prison I long for, the past is a holding pen,
the past is eternity because I did not die then.
Now youth breaks out of Kreuzberg & Wedding, out of
    Pankow

on the east side (side no longer), flows unchecked
across the border, smashes the rest of the broken wall even,
to widen the space
                        & something in my old heart
wants to stop it, wants to retain
the orderly street, the fading State
offices, gilt-scrolled windows, resembling
banking rooms, that defined my ordinary
middle-aged eternity, my stroll, wants to
put the Wall back. As if time would stop,

as if when I went to Vancouver next week there might
be a Wall, a part of the city I could not enter except
by passing through the approved crossing-point
    (Broadway & Clark),
answering personal questions, giving bona fides of my
    existence, then emerging
on the far side, the good side, the dream side,
knowing myself to be a good citizen, inspected therefore
respected, & that the State (either of them) would protect
    me
from death.

If the young can be kept from knowing their power
(which is the power of time), if they can be made to accept
the reigning system, one memo, one regulation at a time,
with its bullshit rationale, then the old will not die.

Then the old will walk the streets of Vancouver & Berlin
fed by the respect that is paid to them by the State,
by the faces in their mirrors, & by the young, too,
unwitting collaborators, lured, conned, into the plan,

the plan behind all plans, the plan to control time.
We need not die (though we are very old), & you may
    remain

60

children, adult children. One more decade, one more year
    of eternity . . .

But the reasons wear thin. Become disconnected
from the hours of the day. And the night. The places
where assent had been given are unattended.

A detour is found. The young see each other, not pictures
of the old. Then the Wall falls. One less memory is real,
    one patch of ground
liberated. And the old must learn that history

is not their house. They must learn, like the young,
to live by their wits.

Three Chinese Men

The poet: one who constantly
thinks of something else.
CZESLAW MIŁOSZ

The three Chinese men, one with
Walkman earphones, passed by the window
of the Greek restaurant on Broadway —

no connection with the poet eating lamb chops,
facing away from the window, toward the bar,
where the owner kept appearing, a smile,
a hint of a question, on his broad face —
Is everything — is your drink — all right?

A fake marble fountain was gurgling,
a bouzouki tape played, the only other
people in the restaurant a young couple,
the girl Asian, the boy white, who seemed
to have just met & were talking softly but
continuously, as if fearful of shared silences —
A blind date? the poet thought, & then unaccountably
turned to look over his shoulder
out at whatever was there — air, wires,
buildings, a street (Broadway),
cars traveling at great speeds, & thought,
It's meaningless (as had become his wont
since attaining high office in the Party),
but looked a little longer,

& then, from his left, along the sidewalk,
conversing (well, two of them were conversing,
the other had Walkman earphones),
three Chinese men. How could there be

men in a no-world? What was the one, the tall one,
saying to the other, & the third, slightly ahead,
what was he listening to? Beethoven?
Chinese opera? They passed by.

In all this nothing that surrounds you,
there was once something, there was mystery,
you didn't know what it was, it was all the more real
for your not knowing.

Then you got it down pat, you got it
fixed in your mind, you knew how to use it,
enter it. You went in & out of it, around the back,
first, where the discards were, then in the front door.
You were it, and it was you, too.

Then it began to disappear, as you will disappear,
poet, eating your Greek food. The owner
comes forward, still a bit hesitant.
'A little ouzo with your coffee, sir?'

The End of Bohemia?

for Liam O'Connor

When Julian Maclaren-Ross sat down alone
in London's Wheatsheaf & asked, Where has everyone
    gone?
he knew the answer was they'd all gone home,
some to earth, some to Paddington. Finally, it was time.

And when Jack Spicer had to shout to be heard
over the goddamn jukebox, Gino's began to fill up
with the kinds of people he'd warned about in his poems,
police agents, *Chronicle* reporters with beards on the soles
    of their feet.

(In Vancouver we had pub night only on Tuesdays.
Nevertheless the management of the Cecil
tried to drive us out, first with country music,
which failed, then with strippers, which succeeded.)

And as you tell it, Liam,
after Paddy Kavanagh died,
some of the old ones held quick consultations
with their doctors, but the young ones
held dinner parties, & gave over attending
McDaid's entirely. (Not to mention UCD
    being moved to the suburbs.)

(But maybe Post-Modernism itself is just a phase,
prelude to an era (as Jameson suggests)
of neo-proletarian uprisings. Then, in the truces,
what colours might Bohemia wear?

64

The Puck

skids on the ice (practically no friction). Sometimes it
rolls — then it's harder to whack into the net. We follow
it. 'Watch Bure,' Daniel says. 'Don't watch the puck — it'll
come to him.' I watch the puck, the black dot. On the
replays, of near goals, sometimes I lose it, in the collision
of bodies, the goalie spreadeagled, the glare. Then it
reappears. Is it in or out?

Second period. Somebody lights a joint. Now it's different.
Watch the puck *for dear life*. The puck *is* life — is like a
word, in conversation, the huge surrounding fucked reality
— sense of your own body, hunched, & the city, doomed
— a terror — where to fall would be to escape it, but you
can't fall, you're doomed, sentenced —

Somebody says something — but before the second
word can open its damp wings in the sunlight, there's a
commercial, cars or beer are pushed in your face,
                                                    but you
can take it, you're committed now (it's somehow like being
a Red Crosse Knight in the service of Una), as you watch
the puck, that has its own life among the players, in the
game (that is worth the candle),

& all about the *cliffs of fall* — smoking dope it's like that's
all there is — the fall you can't fall, because you remember
yourself & forget the puck, the word, & then you truly
can't fend off the commercials, the car drives into your
head & is wedged there, & the beer pours through your
veins —

You are like Prometheus on the rock, & the car, the TV set
with a car for a head, the pterodactyl, is eating you, & you
can't fall.

65

Third period. Now the beer is heavy in your brain &
the dope keeps calling you back to your damned self.
Nonetheless you know what you must do, keep your eye
on that skittering black blur, on what is between us & has
its own life —

for when you think of nothing,
it gets by you, you miss the pass

•

The word — the butterfly — its path — its road —
depending on so many — in the ambient — in the
ambience — winged — when it is set free, from the lips, we
(who hear it) are set free, from ourselves, to follow it — for
courtesy — not *out of* courtesy, but *in* courtesy — taking
part — taking *parts*, as in song

In the beginning was the word — a definition of eternity —

& so that's why you can't interrupt (Dale berated me
in cold anger at the first Adad salon, 'So you want to
interrupt do you, you have to say something do you, so say
what you have to say,' & when I said I'd quite forgotten,
tried to pass it off, fiercely, 'No, say it!') because the word
has just begun its ascent,
                              & promises to take us, carefree,
with it, & our own words can leap up & play with it, so
long as they don't injure it
                              but to interrupt is fatal,
it's like a plane crash. The word is eternal but it can be
killed, like Jesus.

•

66

The puck is different. You can't cross
the river   you can't cross
the blue line   ahead of the puck

•

Decentered — the word is like some never-before-observed
beast — though you can't observe the word, you can hear
its whirring — the one who speaks the word — who *first*
speaks it,
     is he its creator? or only one who
finds it — lost in time — restores it to its birthright? — but
it had its birth elsewhere — the little child.

For the word to — the word is innocent, like the child —
Bowering wrote of the poem as *boy* — for the word to fly
— eternally — like the puck — it must be spoken by one of
us — set free —
     so while our minds (for their own sake)
are on the word — our hearts go out to the speaker — she
— who put herself on the line — the blue line — risking a
slow whistle —

•

The puck has to be kept in play. The puck is only a round
of hard rubber — a black bologna — frozen
         doubly frozen,
when trapped against the boards by skates or sticks, or
under the sprawled torso of Kirk McLean, out of sight. The
ref has to put it back in play, at the face-off, drops it. The
two players whack at it — off it goes— that is what makes
hockey the kind of game it is.

Thomas lights a joint. It is late in the third period, the
Canucks are behind the Islanders or the Blues by 2 or 3

67

goals. Suddenly I am centered again. I am the puck (as Barry became the Centre, for a terrible moment.) It is all about *me* — history, this moment — the other players (what do I mean, 'other'?) are frozen ghosts — unless one whacks me with his stick — but inside me, there are players, too, whacking me, as I go skidding down the ice of time. What a story! How to escape it!

•

How to escape being the focal point of history. Each one is stripped, like Jesus, of his garments, the cloth that tied him to the others. How to keep the others from fading. Our hearts go out to you for your willingness to speak — to be willing but not to will — to be on the lip of — the cataract — to be spring — where what was frozen can melt — where the child can appear —

the child the word the bird the butterfly the puck. They have no need of us. They keep repeating (unless the entire system of our love closes down, leaving us only these games —

But where our care does go, where it is wanted with a chemical hunger, is the willing, dying, speaker

After John Newlove

I'm approaching it from the wrong direction, & so I don't
recognize it. Someone — that's as basic as you can get —
someone is who we are. Someone arrived, just a moment
ago, from the previous moment, where not-he, not-she,
had spent a century, an eternity, but then not-his, not-her,
lease was up, & someone had to skedaddle — & arrived
here, not knowing what it was not-she, not-he, confronted,
was over against, because not-he, not-she, approached it
from the wrong direction.

If this is the world, then where am I,
what is this loneliness, this outpost?
Or if I am not I, but only someone,
then there is nothing I am over against.

Finally we all face this together,
but don't know what it is, even
though no longer approaching it, in the heart
of it, in our hearts, but still, somehow,
from the wrong direction.

From someone's heart.

The City

I don't want to walk on Granville Mall   walk past the
children   hear their eyes read my thoughts   They
crouch in entryway   squat or sit   legs
skinny   unfed   shaved head & tattoo, pierced flesh

Suits go by, briskly   The children
read their thoughts   or vacant privacy   heads turn,
eyes lowered, fingers meticulously roll a smoke

Voices corroded, raspy   worn by the effort of denying
despair, just for a word or two   the words muttered,
laconic   (like signals)   spoken when needed   for
practical reasons   (except when the demon of rage
breaks free)   Is it   not to let
the mortal breath catch the contagion of
analysis?   If you found yourself
saying something you took too long to say, using a
conjunction, say, *unless, but, nevertheless* —
cut the crap!   unless   unless you had to
get past the sour facts
                          as if a suit,
or a nice middle-class lady bent down &
extended her hand for you to place your foot
on — the first step — up — & say all the
nice words — *unless, it wouldn't have, if only,*
I never
          It's not those words we live
by, but the unspeakable ones — maybe they can be
kept true by shouting them, like the
ultimate, *not!*
          They read your thoughts —
how can you live, caring only about money?
how can you live, not caring about caring?

70

how can you walk by, carefree, thinking
about cars, jewelry,
your mutual funds, security?

The orthodox say:
Human nature is a mind that grows in a baby's brain,
& learns to compete
(As these children's bodies are starved)
                    compete compute consume
(As they huddle together, you stand apart)
                    compute
(As they seek to be friends & overcome bad feelings,
you seek to overcome weakness & be secret enemies
of all you smile on)
                    compete compute consume

By the towers the children sit, naked
By the towers, with black stick legs,
torn cloth, tiny holes in the mesh

The towers rise   of steel & glass
up over the streets   in the carpeted suites
the shadowless light   the fine, filtered air
cleansed of static   the molecules, polished

the suits stride back & forth   & get paid
for their faces   their eyes
are information receptors

the hand is an information receptor
(the hand is a starfish, the information enters
via the mouth)

You have to have more than five senses
to keep ahead of the world — up here

I have a profit-maximizing module
implanted in my hindbrain, it
overrides family values.   The data
is sorted, screened   the little things
fall through the screen   finer & finer
screens   the little things fall   the trays
are emptied   into the clouds

I have the finest of minds — compete, compute

High above the children with their stick legs
red spots of anger, white faces

new towers rise, cranes ratchet up their sides

at the top, a visual racket

Poem Enclosing its Dedications

& now I'm looking at someone
in a T-shirt, who comes out of the shade
of his apartment & wags his fingers, briefly,
against the steel frame of his glass door
so they flash white, in the sun.

The sun makes the apartment building opposite
reflect the light, off its paint,
dirt-streaked.

Two trolley poles skim past (the top halves).
The wires sway
                    for Judith Copithorne & Daniel Ignas
The hemlocks or firs or whatever move slightly
in the breeze
                    for Renee Rodin

Another man in a T-shirt gets out of a grey car
(I don't know the names of things —
trees, makes of cars).
The blue sky says nothing,
but what would you expect it to say —
do you think that behind it there are wheels?

A man with a yellow shirt & a
yellow cap. A blue truck. If I don't know
him by name why should I know the truck's
family?
                    for Barbara Munk

A lyric poem.
A man in a brown vest & a T-shirt
carrying a plastic Safeway bag.

The traffic signal sways.
                              The blue sky means the sun
is warming Vancouver.
                              Another bus,
this one going west, to Dunbar or UBC,
so I can see the full length of the poles.

Maroon car. Man in blue jeans & grey
sweatshirt & black helmet on a bike. Another
guy on a bike. Woman with raspberry red coat
walks up old concrete steps with a Safeway
bag.
        Red car.
Cherry red. Wild cherry.

Four people, one pushing a bike.
Green sweat, white helmet.

Man sits at desk, looks out window at
cream-coloured apartment building, parked cars,
conifers he doesn't know the name of, only
knows they're conifers because he can remember them
greenblack in winter — at trolley wires &
thicker black (hydro?) cable, sometimes birds
sit on, crows, pigeons —

old '20s 2-storey gable-roofed house on
Trafalgar, Avalon milk truck, blue
sign of Westside Ski & pink sign of
Montri's restaurant

& blue sky all behind this. Sky blue.
Sits writing poem. Wowowow of ambulance.
Stops.
        Stops writing. Poem goes on, world goes on.

The Young Monks Understand Eternity Better

for Jay & Pete

The young monks understand eternity better,
playing with their dogs, repairing their bikes.
For them sunlight is sun, not a phenomenon,
& rain rain —
                    they seem to have bodies
between their minds & the outside world,

while for the old fox the rain starts
in his heart, as it did for Verlaine,
& he feels responsible that it rains on the city as well.

Brightness of brightness   the young monks sing
like O'Rahilly   the old Cork poet

& though the rain on the city can make it rain in their
    hearts,
it never works the other way, as it does for the fox
for whom the rain starts in his heart . . . (etc.)

And when the sun shines,
brightness of brightness sing they
like the old Cork poet O'Rahilly

(but the fox remembers the Corkery history
that the brightness is of a dream, a legend, a vision,
& he sings, contingency of contingency,
knowing the sunlight to be insubstantial,
a visitation   of energy
of the universe   an accidental, phantom universe
that is in fact no more than is signified

by the words *sunlight* & *universe*
in the philosophy of Wittgenstein, Rorty, et al.

& that having deprived the world thus of any reality
we put language on a pedestal, a plinth . . .

Well, if the Sun were to walk into my room & address me,
sure I'd believe in him, I'd be a young monk myself
for whom language is trash, like yesterday's *Province*
with the lies from Bosnia & the true sports scores,
lies & truth together, indistinguishable,
put out in the blue box to be recycled
(though the city is rumored to deliver them secretly
to the landfill, there being no market
for mixed (& indiscriminate) lies & truth —
until the old trees are cut down, killed,
        to make toilet paper
& forms for pouring concrete for the skyscrapers
        of Kuala Lumpur
                              all which the young monks
dismiss, disdain, it has no reality
compared to the brightness
        & warmth of sun breaking   through shriveling
        rainclouds, & coming into the kitchen!

The young monks ride their mountainbikes
        & rollerblade
& ski
        in a world forever unnamed, or
        rather one that eludes naming, as
miracle upon miracle it reveals itself

(I'm not saying the young monks have no feelings,
no doubts, no fears, no dark night of the soul —
only that their unnamed bodies keep their
        minds from intruding
on the palace of the sun, the rollerdrome of the stars

76

Abner

'I'd trade places with him in a minute,'
said the young monk, of the chocolate-speckled
Catahoula hound rolling at his feet.

'You don't think much of being human,' said the old fox.
'No, I don't. You do, but you're an artist. Without art,
you're an animal.' And was out the door, dog at heels.

That hound is Abner. He lives at the monastery
with four other dogs, one a white female boxer pup
with a brown eyepatch, the other three bipeds — monks —
& Abner sniffs them all every morning
to know them — sometimes several times in one morning.
(It's not just recognition, there's more novelty in it —
as there is in the morning.)
                              Meanwhile the rain — the
hail — of information continues. The monks sit at the
   kitchen table,
reading the *Globe & Mail*. It tells them
how stupid they are not to understand
their true nature. 'Born to compete, boys.'
('Born to lose,' say the monks.) 'It's not just
the bondholders have you by the short hairs,
it's your attitude.'
                    If the *Globe & Mail*
could be translated into doggish, would Abner wonder,
'Compete? for food? for love?' Abner fights
with Dess, the boxer, for chewtoys, tug-of-war
with the old mophead, but that's just play,
not dog eat dog.

The monks compete. They compete with monks
from other monasteries.

The dogs howl when they're gone —
howl with loneliness. They don't know what time it is.

Hours, days, months, centuries pass.
Then suddenly the door opens. Ecstatic,
the dogs leap up, try to climb the monks,
lick their faces. Abner is so happy he wags his tail
so hard there are blood spots the whole length of the hall,
Abner-height.

The young monk talks to him.
'If my arms were forelegs, if my hands were paws,
I'd drop to the ground & be a dog like you,
I'd sniff the world.'
                    (But whose world would it be?
the old fox thinks, emerging from his den.)

'But you'd just like to be up here, reading the paper,
eating your dinner with a knife & fork,
& talking away, like me.'
                    The fox thinks
it's not exactly the moment to defend
humanity, or the dog's dim desire
to escape eternity, such as it is,
when he himself has been drinking whiskey
& reading philosophy, to get down.

Return of the Abbot

for Leo Cooper

'The monastery cannot be destroyed,' said the abbot.
'I have planted a dogwood tree. It is illegal
to cut down dogwood trees. Therefore, the monastery
    cannot be destroyed.'

'I didn't bother to tell him,' said Fra Pietro,
'that in two years his dogwood tree will still be a sapling,
    not very tall.
The new owner will have it dug up & wrapped
with the dirt clinging to its roots & some added dirt,
in burlap, & hand it to the abbot, saying:
'Here's your tree. Now get the fuck off my land.'

The abbot returned home on Sunday.
He brought a bottle of Jameson from the duty free shop in
    Amsterdam,
& gathering about him the monks, friends & supporters of
    the monastery, in unsolemn conclave,
they drank the Jameson, & two cases of beer,
& the abbot smoked a pack of cigarettes, & two joints,
& made about thirty phone calls. And when everybody
    had left, or gone to bed,
the abbot cleaned up the kitchen.

Today, the abbot being 'without wheels,' left on the
    stagecoach
for 41st & Arbutus, to drop in on the landlords.
The abbot is chairperson of the tenants' committee.
(The monastery is only one of several tenants in this
    1920s-era corner retail–residential property, others
    being a hairdresser, 'retro' furniture store, art students.)

79

No formal election was held for this post.
Everyone knows the landlords
expected the return of the abbot
& knew the committee would not be formed
until he came back.

Now, in the middle of the night, the abbot
enters the monastery again,
festooned with 12-packs. Behind him,
dark against dark, the bowed heads of two

novices.

The Power of the Unhappy People

The unhappy people have great power.
They invest in the unhappiness of others.

Not generic unhappiness, the kind
of unhappiness anyone could feel,
but designer unhappiness, the exact
shape of the hole in your heart.

These are dreams without doors. Let the blonde
demonstrator slip one around your feelings.
As it goes on, it clings like shrink-wrap.

Now the birds can cry in the night, and you
won't hear them. Or your ancestors. Or jazz.
The image of your death will dance for you
with as many veils as you please.

In your fog-coloured room, in your Queen Anne chair,
you may wish you were dead, but be glad of that wish
since it sets you above the common sort
inured to ordinary unhappiness.

And we, the investment community, will grin.
(Though, like you, we cannot feel the sun or hear the rain.
Or jazz.) We will grin at the though of you dreaming.

More & more people must become rich & unhappy,
so the original unhappy people can die rich.

A Man

for Meredith Quartermain
in response to 'The World'

The cup didn't break (I prefer to think),
only jumped, jiggled, when his fist hit the fake
woodgrain table, as did a couple of pencils,
a plastic ballpen, a paper clip. 'Shit,' he said.
To no one.

Fragments of a thought. Age, experience, destiny.
But strike that last one, for one who believes the universe
has no purpose, he has no purpose, walked
(well, stepped, a foot or two, in an eight-foot cube)
to where the windows ought to be, & stared.

The mountains have some kind of eternal — rejected
several complements, majesty, bare quality, finally
settled on aura, he mused, at least to those
who call them mountains. The earth is as smooth
as an orange, said the devil. He let that one
go by. They were gods, or the habitations of gods,
so we (thinking, men) could crawl between earth
& heaven, at least that.

Sky gods, she said, looking up from the stack of papers
she was marking. So that was out, too, taking refuge
in stories. The whole stratification slipped,
toward the intertidal zone, the female soup.

I could identify with my breath, he thought.
This skin, this lexicon, but a bag, the eternal
pastry tube . . .

82

Outside the Kingdome

Outside the Kingdome a guy with a UCLA
Bruins T-shirt & a cap of some other team
wants to be part of it. This big vacant space
we've come to love because it gives us vantage.

How to cheat Death except to build Hell
outside its gates, after the game.
The ticket stubs & other stuff
blown idly about, by the teenage wind.

Sex at 62

for R.

His head bent toward me, he demanded,
'Lots of kissing, when I make love' — I could
let my mouth be devoured, I could be held —
back & forth rocking, from being held —
& his arms, his hands, all over my body,
admiring its smoothness. I said, no, yours
is smoother, mine is horny, scaly as a
reptile — it was in these moments of talk,
a gift, a joke, the rocking stopped —
we were falling (through the bed
it seemed, the drugs were wearing off),
into some kind of knowledge, unspoken,
this physical syntax —

I knew him, then all through the morning
as we sucked & kissed & caressed
that it was him, got ahead of
this jerky demanding need to *do*
sex, when it was him there was no choice,
only a face, his rough chin, tousled hair —
then we sat in the Naam eating cereal,
his face & neck white, & the black overcoat.

The fear & the demand, to *make* love,
are still here, but the mythology is gone —
the fear & the demand weaker, & desire
weaker — but that it is him, that is
stronger, that the night lit up from inside
the cab when my arm turned his not-
unwilling face to me & the body answered —

84

he was (is) conneccted to the night, the city —

The cock is a torch, a light,
that lights up the body & our bodies light up
the night —
              I can see the end
through him as I kiss him goodbye
at the bus stop, but the face & the words
& that it is him, that shines —

What else — oh that he was Stephen & I
Leopold & the hours were also rooms —
the bar & the taxi on Hastings & the bedroom —
lighted — moving (losing it, touching,
knowing, losing it)

towards the mouth, mouth on mouth,
      the mouth warm wet,
dark red the lips around, the dots
of beard, the eyes that would suddenly
open to see me & seductively close,
      deluxe,
the lighted-up minutes, desire breaking
through fixations, making me
glad I'm old, glad they don't hold
no more, letting him, body against mine,
turning & turning over — but going
too fast — doing too much too fast — not
loving the time, slower, better next time

never get any closer

Robson St. '97

On Robson planet, you have the right
to place your foot, well shod —

The madman recites the words of a song
in a horrible voice & stops walking, stops short,
to make his mad point, that the walkers are thoughtless —

It's not a stroll, or a *paseo*, it's a
determined pace, they pass each other up,
the boys in muscle shirts walk three abreast —

They're on their way to the very near future,
the rainbow veil, when the street & all its people
resolve into a phrase, or a fashion,
something that is happening everywhere,
but also not happening —

happy without happening. No country for old men
hiding in their T-shirts — all this summer —
summer on Robson St. — yet cold
& without passion — without person —

the condition of the beach resort
brought to centre city — bodies full of meaning —
police on horses —

Long past the documentaries.

2

Mountains & Air

1. LIGHT UP THE WORLD WITH YOUR FAITH

To build up a world out of strange books
in the absence of faith. Going to the store
for a pack of cigarettes, going to Prince George,
going to sleep, exactly the same

trip. The hardest step on every journey
is the last, and every step is the last,
downwind from the engine. Yet
    every one of us expecting

(as in a cornfield) realization,
the answer ripening to the question.
To have them both, the breath of hope

in air. After harvest it is impossible
even to lift your feet. The police
shouts in the night, shouts in the brain
    the voice,

tiny but confident, as each grain
is eaten. Answer to answer to answer,
lined up. There is nothing to do with this
but put up with it, live with it. Paper
your walls with it.

2. 27/10/76

Where to get back to the truth
I don't have the truth in my hands

any more. These little stories
don't even need the language,

89

they use the peril language.
Deep in the middle of everything.
Germany. Your picture of the Saskatchewan
     Wheat Pool.

     3

The mist rises
off the river.
The bears come down
to eat the garbage

back of Dog'n'Suds.
Stand up in the road
like little boys
in bear suits.

This is Big Rock, this is
Carwash Rock,
early in the season

     4. LAKELSE AVENUE

No look back
          when you
get out to the edge you see
nothing.

I was born into a world
of appearances, sub-
stantialities, soft
colours, sharp noises,
clouds closing. It
had a rattle.

Nothing has no name
you
    fight to get back
to the familiar
          turns
of phrase, the triang-
ulations of recognition,
the quantum jump

into the next block
under street lights
ask for a cigarette,

the town shimmers,
trembles.
    Feed this
grinning transparency.

5. TELL THE TRUTH

Learning to live alone, learning alone
Why? Because there is no other
person yet? No, there may be.
But all seem alike to me, other
than me, not other to me.

To make me up, that was the way
then. Now made up, trimmed
of useless branches,
     foliage hanging
over the road, a good self
but off the road, a limbless
self, good wood, no knots
in me, a pole.

Learning to live alone, learning alone
to live? In Terrace?

I don't know why I'm here unless it is
to be here.   To be *here*.

Oh yes the job that I deserved
like a poker player with a run of bad
luck deserves a flush, & BC Med
is my hole card, which I find contemptible.

My dreams make no sense to me,
    they seem to be
about things I have never heard of
My daydreams too. Someone else
I seem to be, not the old familiar me,

& I'd gladly believe life was a cabaret
or a carnival, or a ship, except that it isn't
This mere state of being is vast

    6

Glaciers in the arms of trees.
It is a topography, it is
a vast shadow.

Drove up the logging road
3 miles before I realized
it wasn't going anywhere.

Hummingbirds at feeders.
Indian boy, hitchhiking. Bus
trudging through the slush, near Kwinitsa.

Ravens.

From all points
they fly
      to one
heart of being.

    7

Big fish on the line,
Kispiox River.
Impossible that this
ever be other.

Too many wooden bridges.
Go slow,
take your foot
off the gas.

Each individual
bear, fanged,
each individual
plane.

    8

What am I forgetting?

    The fear

that grows from the centre
of a person's being. The fear
of death, the fear of woman

transmuted in the clouds
into a fear of flying,
the engines failing,
the wind's fingers. And yet

the bird escapes the wing's fingers,
soars upward, falls

is caught
by law

by uprushing air

9. FEWER

cigarettes (marijuana), more
cigarettes (nicotine), more
wine, less beer, more coffee,
less tea, more whiskey, less

swimming, more flying, more snow.
Up there I want to be down,
down here I want to be back

home out of mortality. ('Wouldn't you
want to be their age again?'
sd the lady at my elbow
    before the framed
photos of the graduating class,
early '70s.) What? When? I gave the
expected answer, no, not all that

ignorance, living in an
unreal future again. But this?

Back down to the motel, to get cigarettes,
I heard my boots crunching across the snow,
I saw the women looking at me, it

gladdened them that one so
handsome, breezy, comes in,
gets cigarettes (I dreamed last night

94

they had extracted the cancer,
a California doctor, charged me
7 bucks & wanted to keep the tissue,
it was dry & spongy in his hand
like dry cod out of a barrel.
I agreed, he could market it
better.

I will come
            to some trivial
point, unable to choose,
the right hand
or the left

    10

The poem wrestles you
to the ground.

Reg takes the plane up.

I argue w/ Ray Tickson
in Rupert,
that night.

I don't need no
rollercoasters.

I thought we were climbing
100 miles an hour.

n tons of metal,
2 Pratt & Whitneys
hurtling up a
grass blade
vector,

        the seats
next to me filled w/
sleeping women, or
CBC brass, staring
straight ahead

    11. 13/1/78

Work Channel,
           & behind it
the peaks, & a loose, orange
streamer of dawn, & the pilot asks us
if we're getting any heat.

The rising air
continually replenishing

Here I feel safe,
even happy, with the water below,
the engines, the radio, etc.
                Why then
does the image of this flight
come back to me

what keeps me awake at night
at the conscious edge, peering
    through vacancy?

I think I can't find my way
back from there, back to the place
    I imagine
as

standing at the kitchen counter with
a woman I love cutting
tomatoes & peppers & drinking
a cocktail?

96

Those mountains
are enormous, every dark stipple
in the snow on their sides
is a tree

12

Hamlet says, this is a place
a point of air & space
connected with the points
I cannot see to reach,
love unquestioned.

More throbbing, that flower of air
bending to hold us
in the white petals
of the mountains

Up the Portland Canal
sliding on the wind
Pilot looks around as if
he felt someone scared

13

There's only these few
various motions
varied

See all the way
to the coast

Above it
lots of room

(he leans around
holds up his pack
of Number 7

okay
smoke

14. SLOW

You see birds, hundreds of them
in an updraft over Mt. Hays
(or Oldfield, can't ever get
the two of them straight) & you think
of starlings
    clogging the intakes
of a jet at Logan.
      Fear tightened
underground industrial lights & rails.
Winking, moving.

Then you see four birds
against the same hill
one of them overtaking
the others. Look

at beauty, try
to remember, try
to fix yourself
here in nature,
you & it & oh

beautiful word, you,
my father taught me.

'You take those treatments,
& they make you sick,'
he said to me.

98

It is the loss
I fear, when the cozy cage
of life we build is blown apart by truth

& in the up-
drafts & downdrafts you find your-
self savourless & only an eye

left, darting.

15. RUPERT WINDS

Rupert winds blowing
the television set
mind out of its socket.

Not winds of thought, they
are stilled. It is the chaotic
Spring Sunday morning,

'the equinoctial storms,'
Marlene Huddlestone calls them.

No particular state of the elements
in itself means more than any other.
Even though Narcissus looked in the water.

The winds of night pour by
disequilibrium & sound
without image.

I feel the look
of the unnamed

& speak the words I have
tenderly:
wind, rain

16. CHINATOWN
for Annyha

The culture whirls by us so fast
we can hardly see
things
we called
supernatural

The culture knows
what it knows
& what it calls
the supernatural
is like fried won ton

A Chinese restaurant
Flying knives

through whose doors we push
onto city streets

Hastings & Main & the full moon
light up
the supernatural

17

Sailing above our shadow
with a lighthouse
sticking up out of the harbour
like a sparkplug

when the soul is un-
agitated & the sweet
pneumatic air
lifts you like a pillow

Granduc mine shutdown
announced in New York.
The news transmitted
to Rupert in tones of
reproach.

Out over Chatham Sound I feel the sweat run down my
    toes.
Am one of those Granduc miners, tied to land &
    resources.
Person without place an absurdity.

What blather, '70s
poets quote
the CBC news. Pick up

Braudel (easy to read
at this altitude, not like
Martin Robin)

Chinese river transport:
'The richer the merchant
the longer the rafts'

I imagine the Portland
Channel to be the Neva
& Stewart Leningrad
1' above sea level

Some part of my mind
wanted turbulence, fear, sweat
so it could get the line

'socks soaked' in the poem
Like Bill Cosby says 'Neat-O'
or Julia Child on Niçoise

chickpea pancakes,
'Socca to 'em!'

Sailing over Tree Point

& peaks of waves

Foam on the channel

Gentle Northern Summer

1

Looking out window at neighbour's spread,
vast spaces 'bourgies' think they deserve ...

(Why judge? What do I care?)

Later, on the grass:

Gentle northern summer, do I face
my uncaringness when my mind
is filled with you? In this gentle time
of trees & bees & clover feel a wordless
reprobation to discover

behind their placed faces & doors
a secret that unites them, willy-nilly,
with the coal trains coming, five years
'down the road'?

(coal dust on leaf & air, in
nostril & ear, 500-mile-long smudge)*

(A mile from the tracks you don't
notice the whistle, in the buzz & hum
of insects & reliable appliances

(Nor 4,000 miles east do New York bankers
coming out the glass doors of their Park Avenue
ziggurats see any coal dust either

---

* There was no smudge; the cars returning from the coal port were
sprayed with a fixative.

103

in the edited texture of events their eyes
pick up

(30 km south my neighbour, F's, pickup
crosses the red cantilever bridge
over the Kitimat River & speeds up the hill
& as he makes the turn at the top, he takes in
the view, of the Kitimat Valley, mountains & mist,
    splendid —
takes it home with him, in fact, it's part of his
lifestyle
        but the clearcuts that hang over us
(like swaths made by the teeth of aliens)
are not part of the 'views' we appropriate,
they are external
           the scraped
slopes evidence value
racked up somewhere, some
big account
        Haul it out,
& then we'll go mining. And the ranch houses
stay put, tame trees on the lawn,
on the crimeless streets

   2

for Daniel

At a table in the old Houston hotel:

'Each time,' Vivian said,
'people got moved out of the way,
Indians, then farmers, then came the mill
& mine, & now (swinging her arm wildly) that mall,
that none of them know what's happening to them.'

104

('The real Trojan horse,' Spicer wrote,
'was Greek sentence structure. The Trojans
never knew what hit them.')

*People of this north will have to change
their ways* (some newspaper)

    Who counts
the changes? a child growing up
in Houston, say, to Indians, bear & moose

(swimming across the river to the hippie houses
& their eyes told / what had moved them)

to teenage void & foreseeing heavy industry
knocking the moly out of the mountains
(not Homer's herb / that kept men sane,
protected from being turned to pigs,
but silver grit that hardens steel for war
to see who will control these malls, these stalls

He sees the bland & bowed consumer heads
in Ali Baba's cave, pass the tumbled piles
of glittery cloth, cold sparkle of death games,
pink Mexican fruit,
their eyes all inward turned
on private catalogues

At the checkout stand he sees
the illusion & the cash
change hands (with thank you on both sides).
The former goes eventually to the dump
(of things that cease to charm),
the cash goes to Vancouver
(by computer),
              & sees, *we* are the natural

resources, that 'mix our hands with the earth'
& drive from mill to mall to spend our pay —
the suckers at the breast of dreams

If all this were brought down
quite suddenly, he'd say
people'd rise up in anger
(but with no world to compare it to?)

(& it done slickly, equipment
moved on site, oiled, the go-ahead
archival by the time the wheels turn)

(& if they dare,
the system, the tangled boundary
(that has no place in what we learn as place)
deflates, at every encountered point
draws back with a gasp at being
unappreciated, dangles some plastic
goodies in our faces, some go-cart
& off we go gaily in the snow
follow the moose droppings

then it swells up again, aggrieved
but deferent, gets to work, pumping

value

3

Looking out the window I can see
nothing of the life I'm buried in,
slippage, moraine —

The ranch houses
like a row of broken columns,

tame trees on the lawn. Behind them,
the half-wild second growth in their hundreds,
hemmed in by the bench. More houses,
in the air, some for sale.
It is so still & dreamlike.

To get one more tankful of gas,
I drive to the pump.
Like my neighbor, I accede
to the coal trains coming,
the rearming of Japan, whatever.

The secret is not in the picture.
It is in some closeup of our lives
that we cannot see, smeared over us
like a recurring decimal.

KAL 007

269 people fell in that plane.*
269 people in terror,
each person in terror. Those who knew
each other holding to each other,
or not. Those who knew no one screaming,
or not. In each person's mind,
hundreds screaming. In the dark,

name,   wife   mother
friend   child   God,   I

madness horror swallow meaning
merciful time swallow madness
'twelve minutes
to crash into the sea
seven miles below.'

Each one suffered this & is now gone.

    •

My writing is very small, we don't
    usually think about
how insulated we feel, the comedy of
    our lives
nestled in the tragedy of our life
in time.

Each one like us,
but unwound of his pastimes,

* On September 1, 1983, Korean Air Lines Flight 007 was shot down over
  the Sea of Japan by Soviet aircraft.

thoughts of the next day, next year,
sophistication of stoicism, instantly.

Anticipation of gentleness,
homeward from NY to Seoul,
hot bath & respectful voices, instantly.

Meditation on pride & humility, instantly.

Now in the seat in the sky in a pliant doze,
now a (passing) moment of uncertainty & anxiety

& now Truth has you, all fiction fades,

& Time you shuddered at when you met him
in accidental solitude, is now your angel . . .

•

The face of this Canadian teenage girl
honest smile on ID card looking up
from sucking wavelets on Hokkaido beach

a feeling wells up unaccountable
in terms of my personal identity

What have they damaged
that is valuable to me?

Her face images a past unrecoverable
a pledge unkept, that to the young
after World War Two

•

From the wound of our incomprehension
blood does not flow, but vacuum enters
that cannot be stanched, because there is no care for us
who have taken it all on ourselves to live
not bereft but predatory, tiger-people

Yet at dawn for a second the nameless one
each of us is is named, by a mother,
is a voice, a cry, that turns elsewhere
anywhere out of this world, out of space

•

Less & less a person
more & more simply a locus, a place
no other body can be, a person-shaped
wave, a continuous invasion
until it is invaded
by metal fire or ocean

•

Pray for the 269, pray for the Canadian girl
pray for the Korean businessman

Pray for the hundreds of millions,
how many will have to crash
before we are all
grounded.

Pub Night

This I record,
that listening to you talk, my mind half on you
& half on the variousness of what you were saying,
    it struck me
that love is true, not just real, not just a
    sentiment.

I was afraid I might forget this, so I grabbed
    a cigarette pack that was lying on the table,
tore off the top, & wrote:
    'Truth has a double
    value: obverse/reverse'

(A couple of days later I find it in my pocket
& I taped it in my writing book, under this
quotation from Duncan:
    'I never made any vow to poetry
    except to cut its throat, if I could
    make somebody laugh.'

(The tab of the cigarette pack has an obverse too,
    it says: Player's   FILTRE
                  You can't beat   Rien ne surpasse
                  the taste of   le gout des
                  Player's   Player's

& by 'obverse/reverse' I mean
one Truth, I hope, not two,
not a scattered, shattered love
falling through endless darkness
but a mystery, plain & simple
as a glass of beer (& needing many

111

of same to perceive, no doubt, but
when perceived, perceived with a
lessening of tension, as something
simpler
      than terror.

Terrace '85

A sky, a sense of place
resumes with winter.
'Terrace is targeted' —
party or bar talk, easy to take
as an insider's story of government corruption,
a million dollars of research fudged
raises easy laughter.

Earlier, the sky was a monitor,
a gauge of whether the car starts
or the plane lands
affects language games. When the wind
bams trees down, professionals seek to dream . . .
tie the word to the history table
& make it squeak.

The last word
when shoulders touch
over the fiddle of hands
(of the two sides)
with coffee, the orange plastic stir sticks,
a baffled half-smile,
as if they didn't mean it
(they didn't have to pull the plugs)
is never a word,

the little idol
on the table of politics
does his skater's waltz
& veronicas
for the beetles of power.

The people leaving the meeting places
looking up.

For some a slightly sharper
outline of the mountains
wakens a dormant system,
a valley, an interior.

Looking up we see clouds, stars, portents.

Looking down we see targets.

•

Where the sky meets the cutbank,
a glint of light to alert the eye
(which wonders, was it *in* the eye?),
an optical effect that attuned me
to the new way of seeing things.

Not a new way, but the return
of an old one, it was the way the world
looked before the last period of dreaming.

Intervals (space between ramparts) of dreaming
may last for months, never
more than a year. They are like seasons, maybe
no cycle at all.

Maybe I just woke up because of some random
thing. Always when I do there's
nausea, at being back in the world again,
& always, also, a moment of self-reproach. Is it
my fault, I ask, my lack of vigilance that
let me wake.

•

In the dream time, in the interior, sky is
just a gauge of weather, of whether the car
will start, the planes land.

In the deepest part of the dream
the tender blue of winter
shows through the overcast
to the south & we
return to the games.

•

The wild animals in the darkened rooms
turn slowly into children when you snap on the light,
more slowly every year, it seems.

My New Past

for Daniel Ignas

'I can go back to my old past whenever I want, to times in
my childhood, or college. But my new past never happened.'
JOY, AT THE ACHILLION

Did we spend four years — a high school
or college length of time — when every week,
once, twice or several days, sometimes
whole days together, we met, hung out, talked,
touched (in that poor-spiritual way
men have), & not a trace of it all
left?

     Not true: certain eternal
moments survive; the first one, for example:
your Panama hat, Lawrence's horse. But each
is a 'treasured memory,' a mental
vignette. The place they were
is gone. Where is North Central B.C.,
August, 1982, at this hour?

Further & further on, but less & less
tied to what went before,
I seem to be journeying. The image is
sand. Peripherally haunted by its
random sculpture, unmoving but shifted

under changing skies. Every morning
I wake to a blank, then deduce
the separation. I used to go,
1968, 1970, 1971, 1974, 1976 —

116

private hopscotch, contrived
for the player's solace.

          My new past
never happened, is not available
for edification. Nor is the present
a distillate. There is some other
kind of causality than history. To take
a catchphrase from the airlines, a
hub-spoke arrangement, each year
a separate outpost of childhood,
no advance.

          And maturity
is getting used
to this scattered country. Who told us
we would cross the River Lethe
in this life?

          Wordsworth and Eliot,
when they got here, & saw they had
no baggage, smiled, & wrapped their loss
in forgiveness.

          Forgiveness of whom?
The child I was, not knowing life would come
to sand & snow? Or my new self, drifted,
encamped, below the mountains.

Terrace '87

High snow on rock a word

I sit in my campchair, aware

Distance is false, all is here
in the sky

Then giant cracks
break the summer air,
courtesy Kitimat Chamber of Commerce

I hear Nechako raindrops falling
inside a mountain,
river torn from valley,
chained, head down, in a tunnel

drives turbines
till pure inanimate power shines forth.

(I see the Alcan shareholder smile,
slitting open his broker's statement.)

At the Inn of the West
(some still call the Lakelse)
the Terrace Chamber, in fern-filled
morning sunlight, dreams:

'energy-intensive industries' —
technology, an elixir —

jobs for 'the youth'
(remembering when they last felt young

sales were up, there was a kid
to boss around the store) — Capital

(Dudley Little* said it years ago:
'Without Columbia [Cellulose]
[now Westar] we'd be nothing')

grant us our lifestyle

•

I see now the young Nisga'a, heir
to skinned hills, rotting stumps
(Tree Farm Licence One)
dance backwards into Greig Avenue
away from the enraged 'white man'
with the pool cue
                    & I think
he's a raindrop
skipping over the land
until he splashes

•

& settler boys
not talking, stand
in sapling clumps
with rockstar hair

or roll along the avenue
on big wheels & cutout pipes
going somewhere

* Mill owner and MLA, son of George Little, 'Founder of Terrace'.

(going where the pavement goes,
to the corner)

trained
        to want

        •

The mill or smelter
a shiny device
to the eyes of Rotary
(on its long coffee break)

Boys go in,
workers come out
with credit cards — neat!

(but it's Sam Clark's* mill,
it doesn't need any workers,
it doesn't even have floors,
it's self-lubricating
(maybe just the occasional polishing rag)

        •

ALL WE WANTED
WAS A FREE RIDE
Is that too much to ask?

All we wanted
was that moment
when you pass

* Title character in Frederick Philip Grove's 1944 novel, *The Master of the
  Mill*.

120

& the other guy's face
is blank
behind glass

Then the blank guy
wants to pass

•

And if the fish flop,
spawning,
on Nechako gravel beds . . .

(José plays a lot of Liszt
lately.)

There are no words for the fish
the Indians said
shared their lives
with us.
Our food comes by truck.

The boys laugh: Maybe
we'll have to fight for this land.
(& their dads think: tourism.

(& their dads think:
the kids don't want to work anyway,
it's what they teach them. Big corporations
have all the money anyway. Let them
create the jobs.

•

Fall. The rainstorm chutes
long logs down the slopes, jams

the culvert, caves the road. Tractor-trailers
stack up. Our food, our body, our lifestyle.

•

December. Coloured lights sketch
houses of family. Arms control descends
like a gift of Titans. Like little pre-Christian men
imagined Thor, or Russian serfs
a good Tsar. Up where satellites crawl,
Star Wars lasers, power'd by earth's rivers, may streak.
Today benevolence speaks, sublunary commanders

& we've never been so far from the stars,
that were our friends.

Death Thing

I'm waiting for the bus
by the Safeway parking lot
(where George Little had his mill
in 1911, give or take a thousand years),

& I'm thinking about this death thing,
how it's outside any context
you can imagine, even one
it's self-identical with, the only item,

but how in thinking of it
we try to place it in a context
so it'll go away. Like the World Series.

            •

I'm waiting for the plane.
I'm halfway through the metal detector.
I can see the mountains,
a small plane landing,

hear Tom Mackay in the bar last night, joking:
'I have no fear of flying. Crashing, yes!'
Norma broke up. We all broke up, laughing dutifully,
in respect for his bravado.

            •

I'm in the Cloud Room, on the 11th floor
of the Hotel Camlin, asking my brother Gerald,
'Who did this to Seattle? Wiped out the street life,
the bars & greasy spoons on 1st Ave. & Pike

that fed Ft. Lewis soldiers in the Korean War
& us in the '60s?' He said, 'Committees.'

That grizzled vomit had to go.
They wanted a tasteful place to live their deaths.
They rebuilt quick, condos, afraid
those Ft. Lewis soldiers might come back,
climb up out of the excavations, snake past
the darkened construction fences, in the guise
of street kids. They did.

'It isn't even an intelligent game,' I said,
'but it's not a simple one either. It's politics,
keeping people in the dark, & like all games,
it runs out. Shit happens.'

      •

I'm in a motel in San Francisco.
Leafing through a business magazine, I come across
an interview with an old high school buddy,
now sits on many boards.

'Sometimes,' Gordon says, 'I forget the motion
when the time comes to vote.'

                    Sometimes
I forget the motion, looking out the window,
thinking of contexts.

      •

Hard to get my head around it,
no way to get my head around it,
my head's in it, I'm headed for it.

124

It'd be life I'd have to get
my head around, if anything.

'To learn that there is no Santa Claus
is perhaps the beginning of religion.'*
Get your head around that, get real.

This context-bound reality you construct,
this facing up to death is just the fading
of the real sense of reality, fading
of the individual. We don't 'have to believe'
the world is for the young; it just is.

* Gregory Bateson, *Angels Fear*.

For Prince George

in memory, Barbara Munk

I'll listen to the news the day I die,
to hear who was elected, & if
the New Jersey Devils won the sixth game
of the Stanley Cup —
not because I care about these things
(truly I care less & less),
but the game is worth the candle,
lit by the candle.

At Christmas, when lovers' eyes meet over the candles,
their though is not 'you', it's pure meaning,
infinite horizon. I'd rather be a spectator.
I'd rather be a spectator than play games.
I'd like my mind to be dumb as a lover's.

Late at night the middle-aged play Monopoly.
One spills a drink. Slurred voices,
a peal of laughter. Like the old
balls & wreaths on the tree, that dully gleam
from the darkened living room, their thoughts
come out again, sure of welcome.

Teenage Boredom Poem

It is difficult to hide the despair
when you look at the children
The teenagers confront a void
they call boredom, I thought what they
faced was a structured continuum

A gap between standardized items
readily identified as hot dog,
breast, car, the question they
ask then, am I normal, is my
reaction to girls' bodies pure
of any personal, is it all done
to me, do I cue in?

(If the number of items
held up for attention
is gradually decreased
(for more predictable
marketing of) do the items
expand to fill up
the mental field, or are there
gaps (connective tissue?

The teenagers have seen
the connective tissue, the wiring
in back of everything,
through the gaps between the receding
commodity universes,
                    they sense,
as if it seared their hearts, the world
(that, early, seemed to tremble
at its inward-folding edges,
w/ mystery & promise), is destroyed,

denatured, intimately torn,
                              what we have left are
agglomerate, components, death masked as
life, backlit, to buy

Difficult to hide your despair
seeing what teenage eyes (so few)
glimpse between the blocks
of commodities expanding to fill
the only dimension of the mental
field, eyes
              dart,
wisps of thought,
images (forgotten beauty, go
back to geometry, leaves,
snowflakes, beauty was known
then (now queer), but minds
give out, give in, too few,
call it boredom, bow heads
humbly to what is, idea,
world, deadly, off limits,
queer, be like everybody,

then look at children,
younger, clear, inquiring eyes,
cosmic wit, peak of evolution,
an influsion of the divine, no matter —
by then the grid
                    will be complete,
they will be turned into relays,

buy hot dog, see girl's breast,
react, quick, buy soft drink,
memory burns
for a year or two, unutterable
longing & loneliness, then moon,
stars, too, are commodities.

128

The Hangover

for David Phillips

There will be more hangovers
The days that danced once
are prisoners, of the years

The seasons shock us
w/ unbidden power, & we drink
when it thunders;
when the land that spins in the stars
speaks
flower & shower
we feel spoken to & drink

& shiver w/ the thrill
of the immortal gift
of recurrence as present
enjoyment, as act

but even on long spring evenings,
darkness gathers,
the day, obedient to the year,
her lips sewn shut & the number off the calendar
pasted on her forehead, steals past

We drink to defy that vision
Time sucks at the insides of our heads,
dries out
our voices

There will be more hangovers
Lonely mortality will walk Quebec St. again
sick of the horror, of the non-being

of love in us (as in a childhood dream
thumbs & arms & ordinary nearby objects
swelled & loomed, ominously, so the soundless presence

of human screams, the clench
of entropy
muffles & deadens the soul

Each one knows his fate on the hangover
not unique, but to be suffered uniquely
It seems unbelievable, fatuous, that we might return
from within the word, from within the flower
The head is concrete, the air waste,
the whole is figured, mockingly
in the knowledge we seek to escape

& escape

Spring '90

This is spring. Mountains know no time.
Humans know time & say 'come round again.'
The snow, falling, fallen, knows no end.

Patches, melting, freezing, melting again,
have no thought of melting away, & the old
grass, newly exposed, is plain:
'I am neither old nor new, don't you see?'

If we could only see, we would never go.
Human time is tearing us away
from a time that if we turn back to it
at every moment says *stay*. This spring.

Terrace Landscapes

1

The mares & colts near the college. The big single-family houses built on sand & gravel, smooth rocks, once below water. Did they want the smell, the farm smell? Some of them might — might be glad — the farm smell connects them to the earth — the earth has no purpose.

•

Fields as long as there is life, weeds sprouting from 'my' land, quick after rain, from stony dirt. But not from the dirt without stones — without so many — strange.

•

Breakfast with Pat & others — I float my idea out of Gould & Bateson, that since evolution is blind it makes no difference if my life seems pointless too — it *is* pointless — so, relax, you're in tune with the universe. But I realize this is too much for breakfast time — a negative Christmas present — & if knowing there's no Santa Claus implies any responsibilities, one of them surely is, no negative Christmas presents.

•

Standing at the bus stop, talking to Steven. Noticing the give & take, conversation, life-activity. The bus comes. We get on, ride downtown, pass the little farms, talk baseball, Canadian culture. I always want to get my theories in.

•

Vancouver — being there — feeling marginalized — out of it. Stan's cracks about Terrace, & not just that but a feeling of being a hick or old-fashioned romantic, someone out of the '60s but not the hip '60s — out of Margaret Laurence world.

Stan & Scott hip to the new writing — narrative. Stan telling me, with a bit of an I-told-you-so voice, Bernstein is replacing Creeley (now retired) at Buffalo — only later do I realize this is a fact in the history of Buffalo — not art.

Disoriented — my idea of myself, as always, to be sharp, wiseguy — & desired — but now, now ageing, not interested in being sharp, smart — not interested — maybe because of the fear of addressing *any* content — that old, sad pseudo-project again — to hide somewhere — let nothing happen — then nothing will happen to me. Imagined to myself not saying a word about self, only answering if others asked, but being interested in *them* — well, I didn't have to be interested, they (Stan) were interested enough in themselves & I heard myself talking again about myself, my mingy facts, dull upcountry concerns, knowing every time I said the word 'Terrace' I was more out of it, marginal —

•

Terrace landscapes — landscapes of heart & mind — not just trees & clouds & straight streets looking south — a long mile — when dark all the 'Terrace-ness' goes out of it, there's just a dark space, a sense of trees & houses & a mile away, low down, lights of a street, gas station & neon of a hotel, as if that were the only street in the universe, all around flat land, then rising land, then mountains. Fog settling over, riding the flat of the airport hill — in the morning rising, restlessly writhing upward, from the river,

133

& following the river, a river of fog or mist atop the real river under.

The parking lot outside the Safeway is the centre, at night a few cars still parked at the north edge, close to Lakelse, maybe the glow of a cigarette, moving.

The imagination of the town fights with the imagination of the land. The imagination of the land is creative, its forms come out of the land, appear out of the hills, the creeks between low hills, stride into the centre. Not Indian, or animal — bear — nothing so specific. Maybe they are geometric, Platonic — they are forms into which the people and animals can fit their dreams.

The imagination of the town is imposed, a ruled pad. The streets are the lines, they line us up. Driving we imagine we are walking, the tree-lined streets (of Manawaka), on our way to the stores, the bank or the credit union, the library, the doctor. A dream of a town out of a primary reader.

City sophistication an added element. When you eat at Don D, exotic foods served by neat boys and hippie ladies, you can lose yourself in the world it creates — imagine Terrace a community in harmony with other communities in a pacified world — the places cornmeal & papaya come from.

More disconcerting, the last vestiges of the local — the Co-op cafeteria — the oldest old men on canes in the sunlight. And that reality isn't there either, disappears when you look back to the Indians, back to the land. You realize you look back at nothing. Again, there is nothing. It is all made up. Except the forms.

134

Start at the same spot, near where I live, the 'horseshoe', called that because the bench makes a horseshoe-shaped bend to the north around the flat land, once farm land, beneath it, extending south two miles to the river, which makes a nearly symmetrical bend to the south, enclosing the place called Terrace.

Across that plain cut the railroad & the highway, and from where I stand, looking a mile south to what the kids call 'Main Street' (Lakelse), there's a tiny cluster of lights, a floodlit gas station, neon bar of something else, a few white gleaming dots. Like it was the only street in the universe — not a very friendly universe either. A bureaucratic moon. Sometimes I think of Terrace as a spaceship. We're 15 light years out on our journey, all 15,000 of us — or maybe we're 75 years out. We've got a standardized Protestant society — malls, churches, schools, soccer leagues — & we don't know where we're going. Nor do we care. That seems an abstruse question. Are we going anywhere? Well, anyway, away from the Indians.

Away from the news.

Now there's snow on the landscape, on the land once farmed, now laid out in the rectangular blocks of an Ontario town (Leacock's Mariposa) on the north side of the tracks, & the same, but more straggly, on the south. When you get down toward the river there are still some farms.

I saw some posters in the CUPE office today, solidarity posters, one from South Africa, showing men & women with their fists raised & expressions of solidarity & determination on their faces. And I thought, these won't

135

convince, any longer. People are turned off by posters with images of people on them. They remind them that they are people too.

·

Sparks Avenue — leads from my street (which is named after someone who lived there) down to 'Main Street.' It's an ordinary street — it has a sidewalk on the west side (except for the first block at the north end, where instead of a sidewalk there's a hardpan trail through the grass, between the storm ditch and the fenced-in yards. I walked down that trail, this morning, on my way to the anti-poverty meeting. It wasn't hardpan, but slick with a little mud and wet snow on the grass quickly melting.

·

The bus broke down as we were making a corner in Mountainvista subdivision. The driver tried to cut it too sharp, the front wheels climbed up over about a foot of snowbank and then the back wheels didn't, there was a loud cracking sound as if the bus had run over a metal box. The driver turned off the ignition, opened the door, jumped down into the snow & disappeared. In a minute she was back, sat down in the driver's seat & got on the intercom. 'Are we stuck?' I said. 'I lost an air line,' she said. 'Can't move till that's fixed.' We were a quarter mile from the college.

Got out on the road, walking north. Heard a car coming behind me & stepped off to the side — a little too far, my boot started to sink down in the snow — I pulled back. The car gave me a wide berth.

136

It was the point in a storm, or a series of storms, when all motion ceases in the sky. The moon wasn't up yet, but there was still light in the sky, a dark greyish blue, some clouds in odd, wind-shorn shapes, light coming up from the mill to the south, too, & the highway. Walking, just a quarter mile, alone, it was like I was back in Wyoming, hitchhiking, when I was a kid (26, but I was a kid), thankful it wasn't raining, there in the lonely dark but not sad to be alone, lone there, because I knew I was going somewhere, New York & even that was a way station, horizon beyond horizon, simply that I was young & it was all unknown & long ahead, that unknownness of life was better than safety, there was no concept of safety, there was, therefore, no concept even of being there, on the highway in Wyoming — I was just part of it, I was just *it*, in fact, no distinction. No distinctions needed to be made.

Ahead was life, that's all I knew. I heard a huge sound behind me, lit up like blazes a truck, cab & trailers came over the western hill & barrelled down at me, blowing its horn, the gust of wind off it almost knocking me down on the gravel shoulder. I walked on, into deeper night. The stars must have come out, I don't remember, or if it was cold, or even raining, though I think it wasn't raining.

I kept walking toward dawn. Cars kept passing me. I would whip around to jerk a thumb and maybe catch the eyes of the drivers, which was hard, because I was lugging a big, heavy suitcase. Around 8 a.m. a black convertible with California plates came over the rise, a single young guy, blond, sunglasses. I yelled, 'Hey, California!' He stopped ahead of me & I ran up & got in. A few miles down the road, doing about 70, we hit a dog, straight on. The driver didn't swerve, held the wheel steady. The rancher came out & accepted his apologies, said he knew we couldn't avoid it. That night the driver & I stayed in a

137

motel near Omaha, separate rooms. I thought we should have slept together, but I didn't ask.

Terrace landscapes or any landscapes. A sound like a train or a plane or a truck. Wondering, for a moment, if life is simpler — oh no, yes, simpler — than I thought it was — are we back where the monk said we started, with the mountains, trees & sky? All the 'head trips' blown away?

Terrace landscapes — another engine sound. An oil-scape.

•

The dark. The fog moving across the field like a, like a. Nothing. Whitish nothing. Not moving. There. So many feet or metres up then the sky & mountain beyond. Swirls at the bottom. Wet, dry. Follows the river, the river exhales, the damp turns visible, in cold, the breath comes from the warm throat — these things go on, these processes, giving, accepting. The trucks come from Vancouver with the meat & fruit & frozen dinners. The people float in the net, their minds go on & off, images of other people & places flash, wink, in their minds, against a picture they all agree is *this place*, earth, they live on top of, land.

Down below dark, out in the air at night, past the techno-lighting, dark. Distant sun, a whoosh of light & heat going past. The giant rock of earth, of home, between. Mirror moon.

•

The light shineth, & the darkness is forgotten. And what the light shines on? And how long does the light shine, before it goes out again, & the darkness returns?

138

Or is there any darkness? Only a world, our world, located on a planet, which we are subjecting to extraordinary stress — the air-borne & water-borne pollution — the noise — the vehicles — the money — the messages. The energy — all of this in light — but in darkness too, no one knows about it, no one sees it, only when the pressure gets to the setting when the light goes on, the problem presents itself — the snow, the war. It's dealt with, more or less, & then the light goes off, the billions of exchanges start up again, not in the dark (except at night), not even in the dark of the mind, but in a neutral space, indirect lighting, minimally furnished, a desk the centrepiece, the desk dark, polished, empty of any clutter — empty. A pure, rich, glossy, rectangular surface. And then the light goes out. No matter. It's time to sleep now. It's time to sleep every moment. Mama's little baby needs sleep. This is very close to the end.

•

Someone, say H. (This is the way it always starts — how else can it start?) It starts with H. H. is a person completely unknown, except that the color of his skin is known (well, his gender is known), & the color of his eyes, his waist-size, the shape of his ears — and then the way H. walks, that is not like anyone else walks, exactly, is it? When he wears a shirt & tie, on the job at Don D, his face can look as if poised on a column, etc. There are many things about H. that are known — many more that could be known — but the person, H., is not known.

Is the world H. lives in known? Is the world H. lives in the world H. knows? Ah, there's the rub. Imagine, if you want to, that the world we know H. to inhabit is the world H. knows he inhabits. The same world . . . located on a planet.

•

Terrace landscapes. Landscapes of the heart & mind
— my heart & mind — mine only? Of the white heart
& the Indian heart, a place intersecting with a scheme,
a railroad, a mill to cut ties, & lay them. To connect
Montreal with the other side of the continent. Part of a
larger scheme, to connect Moscow, Berlin, Vienna, with
the coasts, to build cities & ports & launch steamships to
connect ports across the oceans. This clearing, this place
on the river, meant for a purpose & when the ties were laid
men looking for other purposes to be meant for (to be men
for?), white men.

Indian purpose? Does it lead into the spirit world, does it
lead anywhere else but straight through your life to your
death & then into the spirit world & back through the
womb — with no merit gained or lost, no rising or falling
on planes of spiritual mist? There were Indians here, not
right here but near here, eyes in the dark, over the crags of
the river narrows, watching the Canadians blast rock & lay
tracks.

•

Snow falling fast as if hurrying to get to ground because
of so much more to come — rough-edged *pieces* of snow,
heaping high over objects — cars & roofs & streets. Wind
coming — coming out of blackness, lifting the last fallen
part, lifting & chasing it, away, against the fence, over,over
the snow-covered street, into yards, up against doors,
living-room windows, & continuing, every time you look,
out any window, to hurry downward, gather, assemble,
rise. Then after it's fallen it has a finished look about it,
as if that was exactly the amount that had been intended.
Now a break. Stars come out, the top of the snow gets

140

crusty. The place now in a way possesses all this snow, like it possesses all the Christmas presents that fill the aisles of the stores.

Kids make snow people. The snowman — a frightening being, if he existed — not like Santa with a warm heart, a human body, but something with no principle of form, heaped together — someone — a being — with no principle. I like to see the snow melt, the sun come out, the heaps decline, subside, the roof-shaped collections of snow on the roofs draw back from the edges, the paths in the snow get wider. The grader comes & pushes all the snow, now without even the form it had when it fell, form it stole from the forms underneath it, and would like to cover forever, pushes it up against itself

2

The real thing now — war.

All the lesser things sort of move back slightly out of focus & take their place in —

Our everyday concerns move back & are shelved — as in banker's boxes — they seem to have some kind of order — they are ready to come forward again — the most important in the first rank — the career plans, or life plans — the relationships — ready to come back into the present, the thoughtless space of everyday living, after this —

& the mind swims — Mulroney's rhetoric, calling on principles of humanity & enlightenment, quoting former prime ministers, doesn't convince but I can feel its power of conviction — Bush's speech less so because the quavery slippery person is heard through the voice as well — but Mulroney's is oratory — & I can feel myself wanting to believe, wanting to be one with him — the nation, the United Nations — humanity — & also with the men & women who are in our thoughts, in our hearts, there in Saudi Arabia & on the ships in the Gulf —

The message — to prefer *peace*, to work for peace, is to abandon *them*, the young men & women courageous, controlling their fear, ready to die

(& in Baghdad, people ready to die)

& in Saudi Arabia, the young woman soldier says, 'Don't worry, it's not as bad as you think at home, we'll all be home.' To stand for peace is to abandon their hopes for peace, & therefore we must stand for war if we want peace & peace if we want a worse war in the future & the mind reels, wavers.

•

And now, of course, we're back in Terrace, restored (that has a faint sense of put back in place, or put in storage).

We're back at the college, in the thick, in the thickets of discourses, prompted by the students, the techie discourse, the geopolitical, the petroleum, the ecology, what of the monsoons? I'm shifting, no, turning, from one to the other, to each person, with her questions, & all the discourses together make a fabric, a textile, something to wrap us in —

It isn't that the war has come home, or will come home, but that we have all been yanked (yeah, yanked) by our strings of media & money & need, by our need for sunlight & food & oil, back into the world, back into the realization (the 'reality') that we are all part of it, all connected.

142

'Only connect'? Only *reveal* the connections — hear how
the skiers are protected, security, the Super Bowl (no
electronic devices allowed), the smoke from the oil wells,
the oil bubbling to the surface, no need to pump, no way
to put it out. Sudan, Libya, Jordan, where is the perimeter?

'I want to die with my friends,' Irv Halperin said 25 years
ago when SF State students asked him why he didn't
return to Israel. I want to die in San Francisco. I want to
die in Terrace. I want to die in a world that has time for
my death.

•

We calm ourselves with language. The media calm us with
language. Behind that soft sound, reassuring vocables,
fine tuning their positions, soft tech, blood.

No blood for oil. For the immortality all corporations
know as their right, that of the military-industrial
complex.

•

Now the war drops out of consciousness, whole hours,
half-days, no thought of war. Then it comes back. Is
'comes back' the way you'd describe it? What happens is
I *remember* (did I forget? did I at some point say to myself,
forget that now? Clear the field, for more important things,
for the freedom to arrange thoughts in your mind like
pieces on a board, but less strictly, the enjoyment is in
coming upon them, thinking them into life, against no
background, the infinite leisure of freedom. No war. Then
it comes back, it's like a fact, no image, behind it images
crowd, the ones from TV, or comic books — planes —
the image — I don't have TV, so for me it's a memory of

143

a newsreel, B-29s over Germany, or the South Pacific, in the closing years . . . there would be more images but the censor — a circuit-breaker in the mind — cuts out. It's like *remembering* you're going to die, remember & as quickly forget — it's like arranging your life so you have only that one thing to remember — and forget.

Peace — a glib term — absence of war — so there'll be nothing to remind us — of man's inhumanity to man — now celebrated. The word is out — the authority — the wimp, Bush — grits his teeth & snarls his words — a soft accent — a grimacing face — a smile that turns into a snarl — genteel — a way to apologize, for not concealing, wholly, the ravening face of power. No pretense it's anything but right makes might makes right & peace is for priests with pious faces but I am a tank I am a gun I am a plane. And the young hear — his cagey, liney snarl is answered by their smooth, thoughtless snarl. It's out, it's free, it's real, it's right.

Peace — a smarmy word — pointing to nothing but the virtue of the one who offers it — cheap — I don't like reality either but — 'People have to die, in war,' the girl interrupts. What good would the peace movement do? What good is peace? What good? Keep your head down & your mouth shut & don't make the enemy think we're not all united behind our troops. If you have nothing to say, say nothing. What peace but peace of mind, & that we buy with — war. Blood. That's why you have the right to have your peace march. So be grateful for it. But get out of the way.

•

Winter 'hanging on' — so many 'knots' her hour, wind at the airport — translates into so many km. Last night the branches whipping, a sound like something tearing was

144

the sudden dashing rain on the skylight. Later in bed, the wind & branches sound reassuring, but why? It always has been. Nature — just far enough away, but there, to say, I am here — not evil — enclosing, decentering 'my' world, ironing out or rinsing or blowing away fear & concerns — make even death natural.

•

Read this morning Carl Rogers at 75 saying he had little fear of death, no more apprehension than he would feel going under anesthetic — and gave his version of Whitehead's objective immortality, that what was of value in his life would continue in others' lives, & after hearing the wind & rain putting my fears in perspective that made sense.

•

Went from place to place today — the anti-poverty meeting, the doctor's office. In the waiting room noticed how many Indians are sick — watched a husky Indian boy playing on a toy where coloured blocks slide on curved rods, with a smaller blond boy. Saw the aggression starting in the bigger boy's face — male, but also mischievous Indian — get back at you — he will some day — try.

•

Reading Emily Dickinson in class. Things that happen make up a day. Rain & wind. 'A slant of light.' The rain starts & stops, the sun almost peeps through.

Before dawn, the melted snow froze over on the shallow puddles, fine, white, crazed cracks — step on them.

Here in class are twenty or so young people writing. In Arabia a war — the world. Peter said, 'I can only say one word — the world is *sad*.' Mentioning various students — 'He's a very good student.'

No purpose. We make up purposes, then we lie in bed terrified of the breaks opening up in the purposes we made — that we might fall. Rain & wind come, cover us with natural noise, the outside. Soon we quit shivering under the covers, fall asleep. There is no inside, no place where purposes & plans wait.

•

Or walking outside the Admin building for a breath of air, the mist-grey world, I think it's just the ordinary ageing, more aware of contingency, of being a six-foot (slightly less) organism, walking on this earth that knows it's not the centre of — no, scratch that — that no longer thinks it's essential to any universe — even fictional. So extrapolating back 30–40 years, I can understand why my students read poems by just glancing at a poem, taking it in all of a piece, & then talking about their feelings. They believe in their feelings, like I believe in the fog or the mountains.

•

The true colour of the landscape, the Terrace sky against the Baghdad sky — another day of bombing while we slept — or no — a day of cleaning up, salving wounds, surgical operations — a *night* of bombing while we walk about in our dazed world, people meanings can't quite get through to —

146

In the Learning Resources Centre this morning two clerks talking about last night's movie, wondering *why* some character had done something — as though it was real —

Also at lunch today, faculty & staff persons chatter of TV, till someone, tangentially, says, 'Saudi Arabia' (with reference to a veiled woman, part of a half-hearted sexist joke) —

Look at the trees as if there weren't eyes, as if *no I*, having to be either a complacent Canadian or some moral critic, the egotism of any possible vision —

Look at the pools of melting snow, the 'lake' in front of the college, fed by the streams & trickles from the black & crumbly heaps, that flows, ever so slow, toward the Kalum. Something reflecting in it, trees, people.

(Another article about the 'economy' that doesn't say it's located on a planet (it's by Robert Reich, out of *Atlantic*), distributed by management, tells us how 'education' (read 'training') fits into some supposedly predictable migration of institutions, moving into the spreadsheet future, carrying or dragging humans in their roles — visualized no doubt (by management) as suspended in space surrounded by healthful brisk yellow sunlight)

('It's just another committee meeting,' Joe Clark said, having had stage fright before his first G-7 meeting, in Tokyo.)

I see a river of blood & garbage moving through a landscape no less unreal than management's utopia — the mainstream, I call it — big trees, rotting trunks, swamp water — & I have pity on all of us spinning around in eddies or in stagnant backwaters or with little rafts of

147

idealism the marines or coast guard keep beating back out of the channel, so the big liners can pass —

The real sky behind the morning sky, the real air, an instant behind the air we think we breathe, the real world ready to pounce on the world we know, that once again eludes its claw, but its reflexes are going.

•

The McEachern decision. The faces of Natives, seen anew. In the mall & the one or two in my classes who come shyly in — when asked to read from Shakespeare they have soft, almost inaudible voices, but they don't trip over words, or race over them, like some of the white boys. I think of jet planes bombing Iraq, tens of thousands of boys dead, like those Hamlet imagines will die in Fortinbras' attack on a 'straw' of earth garrisoned by Poland, *which is not tomb enough and continent / to hide the slain.* Today napalm reported, the jellied gasoline shot from helicopter gunships, but in the *Sun* the letters say we should or should not approve according to whether we're pro-American or anti-American. Language slipping sidewise, to evade the point, any way, not to answer, respond, but to speak again, shift the ground. The Natives are to blame, McEachern says, for not having grasped the opportunity, always there, to become part of the mainstream.

And where is the mainstream, is it the stream of 'goods' that flows from the mall to the house & garage, & from there to the dump? And how to grasp it?

•

Valleys. Looking from the air at the snowdrifted mountaintops no one, no goat even, has set foot on, in

148

niches the glaciers, in the valleys the crooked lines, like pen & ink, of streams, the grey curves of highway. Then encapsulated, riding, at a comfortable speed, home.

•

Look up close. Trees in a Margaret Avison poem

ragged on the windward sides . . .
prepared
for onslaught when the obliterating
blasts sweep in again

Let the trees stop the words, let them stand in front of the 'decision', immovable, at least not movable by language, bendable by wind, but returning to their growing space.

3

Geese in Frank's Field, black/brown/white: black necks, brown wings, white chinstraps. I rode in a bus past the field, I wanted to remember their colors, & the placement, & saw the geese hunkered down in the field, in pools of melted snow, sodden earth.

When the geese come 'home' or 'north', we feel complimented, start to smile on their return. Winter dies, willingly. Its last, left, nothing is now but everything unnamed & surviving. Lasting. Like the black necks, white-ringed (memory swoons), brown-feathered, the blue, the white, the wet, the calm, the oval, the ovary, the delta. Escaping. And all flowing away, the incline, the trickle on that slight gradient of the cool seeping from under the grey, cold, evaporating, upward, the skillful pools, the turning. Bugs. Birds. Sodium. Let live. Shadow on glassy, of the tall, bending, & then the blue again, & the

149

white scudding, & then the geese flying over & the sound, undescribed. No feeling. No one to feel. The slight sound of coughing.

There is such a wanting in all things whether one or many, to be free, & whether part of a separate, & whether entangling or loose. Untouched. Unknown.

•

Spring — a raven sat in the shrub outside my window — heavy bird, bending the branch as it pulled with its beak at a twig — the day before two ravens — then flew away, low over the roofs of the big ranch houses to what's left of the bush, trees & shrubs, under the bench — where do they nest?

What do we do? The snow goes, the many changes that are spring (don't list them) appear, & in that turmoil *we* — is there a *we*? I don't mean people, I know what we do as people, *down to an art* they say, Wittgenstein wanting macaroni & cheese because he had it yesterday — treat time like space, ride herd on vagrant thoughts ('that way lies . . .') & somehow take yourself off like armor, play naked, & deny deny deny at the mind's battlements. So we do this to do that to do naught. But that's our sickness, that's our daily tread, happy are we when our there is here — but that's not what life is up to. Oh, I know, sick feeling, to recognize again, life's up to no good, just up. The where we (yes, there's a we, we're all wee — stupid pun) are is not in my living room for instance, when I stand there I'm not there & if I were truly there I'd be a terror-shape. Like Snoopy trying to be like a tumbleweed, after a few tumbles he gets the point. Better to be intent, & call that a tent.

•

I thought the night before about a huge lament I wanted to make, how I could only express my feelings about the inevitability (which isn't even the right word, more the *certainty*, as Dr. Rank, in *A Doll's House*, says) of death by a list, of all the things in life, tumbling over one another, like out of the Horn of Plenty or Santa's sack, one after the other, pleasures, visions, sky, spaghetti . . . let's face it, there's nothing you can say, or write, about that except that it's nonsense, it's going under . . . and yet it's the only thing you can write about, it's the only thing that stops language cold, up to its tricks, as always.

Language bouncers off death & for a fraction of a second, at least that long, is stunned, & stays where it is (spaghetti for instance) before it bounces somewhere else.

Meanwhile the geese inhabit the field, with their eyes that see a mile ahead, unnoticed.

•

A little substance, solidity, comes to spring with these first after-supper hours when it's light. Not that tentative, pre-adolescent, that March tension. The 'braided' rivers, the channels, making braids around the oval, tapering sandbars. The valleys were once filled with water, the glaciers extended. Now there's less ice, & less water too. That's odd — seems as if the glaciers melted, the rivers should rise, but they don't melt, they evaporate, & the rivers come from the snowpack, which comes from the ocean.

•

The boys with kerchiefs snapping their skateboards up on the dividers in the McDonald's parking lot, across from the bus stop.

Union Hall

If the old are allowed to be young,
the young must consent to be old.

The actual time in Ireland must be
23rd century.
So far in the future to remove
the apparent present
into the deep past.

The flat façades & the shields of the breweries,
the housefronts painted the softest of hues,
yellow & blue, pink & redpurple,
but at dusk all Irish houses are grey.

The pub is a cell of joy,
honey-whiskey light & smoke,
& narrative hilarity,
& truly, no other life
's available.

A Trip in Ireland

A poet among poets — one of the poets — with James & Jim, Dennis O'Driscoll & Philip Casey. One of many poets — one of all who are here — this one of all of us. No trepidation here in Ireland (look that up). No fear of the moment, the time (now) is safe in the past. Our deaths are after, not now. This moment is always (& always) reclaimed by the symbolic, by the falling of words into place (like dominoes?) — like leaves. The words carry the urgency, shoulder it, it's their own. The soul is relieved ('My burden is light'), & the body lies down, laved in the *river of life*, with just the sense organs protruding. Like a hippopotamus.

& what is lost, if everything is not compulsively decorated (a boy just came to the door selling prints by Young Irish Artists), but if the walls are left blank or a clutter of coins, ribbon & train receipts on a tray, they casually fell too, like leaves. Nature must not be kept out at all costs as in America. A huge crack runs the height of the window like a stem. Space left to rise like bread. Mr. Finegan is one of the New Formalists.

So when I came here I felt sinking layer by layer — 'into the bog,' one said, but it was only the companionable (Creeley's word — Irish Creeley) — arrival at Inch — pint by pint — Kavanagh knew — how not to die — breakfast after dark — then to Rafferty's.

Walked around Dublin Zoo — clockwise — the animals watched me, & were quick with their tricks — the giraffe with those knobs, the cheetah posing (no strap), bears acting Canadian, i.e., feral, like Americans back from the wild, like Robert Bly's neo-men. 'The time of men is gone,' James proclaims, in — what was that bar? — and 'sit down, I'll get it,' & later, musing, 'The ham was fine.'

& the train took me, rackety-rackety, to Cork, as the elegant Killarney woman seduced, verbally, the young North Carolina golf pro: 'How many members have you in your club'? 'It's a public links.' (Look that up.)

Time doesn't all run one way. Time, too, has a geography, has caves, & you can climb down into time using only your naked toes & fingers & carry a small light bulb in a wire cage on a string around your neck, & that is sex, explosive as Miss Universe thighs or the angel in Waterstone's with the knapsack that pulled his T-shirt sleeve high on the right shoulder & his lazy rope of gold curls as he moved from Fiction to Psychology — I could not lift my eyes — I remember thinking, he's too big for me — too big for all the dark-haired, short, wide-faced ageing sweating youths — & their sisters — & the odd priest with leather satchel, running to catch — & my cousin crossed himself as he neared crossings, & crossed himself as, it seems, he thought of hate or injustice — liturgical —

all the tiny bottles, the cordials, & Cadbury's biscuits

'Will you have the last pint with me?' And the angel moved in & out of consciousness, still ungraspable.

Arklow

The stunned faces — the stalled lives

A battle no one knows is going on (on 'our' side) —
no one cares to fight. The pub a nursery,
here lessons in intricacy. But they sing Paul Simon
songs instead of the old
uprising, insurrection. Here a priest died.

Their furniture will save them. The carved & polished
& inlaid interiors of the nursery. Whispers behind
whispers. 'They'll look you straight in the face
& never say a word. In Wicklow. In Wexford
people are friendlier. They'll start up a conversation
with you' Soccer its own world.

McDonald's no more invasive than Coca-Cola logos
melt in the cuban syntax, crammed & cluttered windows
& then a big, bare space. Light falling across the faces,
made for the occasion. The boy telling the man,
agitated; the man listens, arms folded, his right
hand to his chin, pensive. All history stops here,
unfolds, for a moment, its medicine chest.

Homosexuality, vegetarianism, green politics. We are
living in the dawn of the old girls' world.

9 p.m. Boys kip, men skip.

156

Coolgreany

To be or not find
motives or interests,
exchanging parts of a story,
some days back, in this 'very' room,
in this house that was part

(& the earth, & all the houses
of parliament, lines drawn crooked
or straight, to demarcate
property, are not re-drawn
again & again, as the universe jigs
from no-being to being

(as the symbolic order
re-flowers in the brain
when a good sleep follows
on a day wasted trying to think
in images)

but they continue,
trees fall in the forest
& you find them later,
true to your disbelief.

You are trying to climb
a sliding cliff, a giving way,
to what you glimpsed through multiple
shifting screens of your own devising
(all of this talk), some real event
that will refract

If being is only taking arms against
phantoms, then suffer, fortune,

& switch on, switch off, mind,
knowing now no world's really there
but something Platonic & personless

Here's a human reality,
unmistakeable — a mouth,
eyes that emit light,
a pulse, a history

The Void

Love it or leave it.

The Aanme

for Peter Weber (1940–1994)

Peter, I see you in your office,
your desk covered with student papers,
documents, communiqués, reports,
& your own memos & lecture notes
off your portable — I could always tell
it was a memo from you by the typeface,
elite, & the single spacing,
& in the memo read your voice, animated,
interpolating apposite data (or jokes about Hitler)
in mid-phrase
                           you were gunning for the henchmen
of capital, in whatever guise —
employers' council, task force on human resources
(that weasel word liberals gagged back
as if there were no difference
between a human being and oil, or a computer)

but if queasy liberals questioned
historical fact, you'd be quick to remind them
human beings can be requisitioned, used,
used up: the corvée, the gulag

& with your hands deep in the clay
of a student's mind, make him say it:
'How did they get them to work in the camps?'
'For food, right!' A smile,
a blinder in the way
of knowledge of power   falls

You taught history as a humanity,
though the historian be a scientist
rummaging in the archives

(Bismarck Hitler Stalin the true experimental-
ists — heads of research centres
(not quite your words
but I think your thought)

     Poli Sci?
'Like teaching English' (a smile
for the English teacher)

Economics — now that was something else —
you attacked the board — neoclassical
curves swooping, the chalk snapping —
to display its sterility
in a single graph —
    Say's law
(& marginal this & that) confuted
by Keynes: the point of equilibrium
is not full employment, but total indifference
to human need (the kids open-mouthed, blank-faced,
or sniggering in the back rows)

Philosophy? 'Sophisticated escapism'
from life — history — at the time of
the Gulf War: 'I have only one word —
the word is *sad*'

quantilla prudentia
*orbis regatur**

•

---

* With how little wisdom the world is governed. (Axel Oxenstierna)

Look up from behind that crowded desk —
a smile of equality, fraternity,
conspiracy (my job —
to get the students to the meeting)

We made you our leader
because you would not play
sectarian games —
'I know *who* I am, now what I am'

You needed to come to terms
with the people running things —
co-operate, & yet, oppose
the satraps of the petty principalities —
Terrace, Kitimat, Prince Rupert —

for education —
for 'working people, Native people & women'
(& maybe One Big Union)

so Don Anderson called you Machiavellian
& you responded, politely,
'Machiavelli has been misunderstood.'

•

Daniel's image, not mine:
'Who is that *teenager*?'
Frame spare as the bike's,
yellow hair flying, sweat shirt & jeans,
whizzing down the airport hill

(mine: pedaling to Kleanza in the rain,
seen from the inbound bus)

•

The state papers of great powers
after war or revolution
are sealed for a generation
(to sanitize reputations)

So you could sit in the backyard in August,
read books, drink beer,
never catch up. In 'this little place,
where nothing will ever happen.'
Except your death.

'I'm going to die,' you said.
And looked   the distance.
And still had a smile for life, for us.

          'The *aanme*,
the personal animating essence
inside the breath. The *aanme* continues
to interact with the living after
an individual dies, and becomes
an ancestor'
(Mayan)

druk, friend

Terrace '79

Driving up into hills of fall,
mottled yellow & red,
or hills of spring, with friends *still young* —
col*leagues*, Peter said, accenting the second
syllable,

that would read together,
look out on the land,
referred to a world long gone
as if that were the world, and this,
on the Skeena, an adventure. Col*leagues*.

Watching us were adult children
of Ontario settlers, whose people
had made a clearing in the bush
by the train track, around 1912.
People with plain churches & unvarnished ideas,
or ideas the varnish had weathered off —
a fine dust of predestination.
Their backyards abutted
on feral orchards.

Watching them were the numerous people
living in the bush, dark & horned.
Hard to see at first, then apparent
all at once, like berries.

We rode up & down the river, we chartered planes
& sent the bills some place called budget.
We imagined ourselves at the frontier
of the imagination (last days of we).

164

Terrace was New York of the North — after hours on the
    road,
a scatter of white lights, dim bulb over the motel doorstep,
quartz halide at the freighyards.

The scientists (Allen & Ian) stepped off the road,
walked up the mountains, waded into the river
(bought hip boots, borrowed canoes
& Zodiacs). Fished,
& up came the fish,
the students, bounding upstream,
up the streams of our ironizing minds,
or idled in the shallows
eddying (Dora's word), to gain strength.

We still young, academic dreamers & misfits,
led their children into the forests of meaning.
Most would go part way only, not intrepid as we
(whose life support came from general revenues of B.C.),
then run back to the highway, charmed by the blacktop
    that led
to parking lots & venues of advancement . . .

In Scotland

Necropolis behind
Glasgow cathedral,

Scottish boys
with soft close cuts.

In Ireland

1. THE DYING COW

My father appeared to me, or rather,
appeared in me, as I was sitting at the bar
in a pub in Wicklow called The Dying Cow.
Appeared in me, shoulders in my shoulders,
lips in my lips, in that attitude
of resignation that marked his old age.

I realized I had long warded him off,
looked in the mirror countless times
& saw my short hair sticking up like his
        from my age-high brow
& quickly brushed it to the side;
felt my lips purse in that small mouth of his
that could not kiss (but admired kissing)
& more & more as he grow old would not
speak, knowing what he had to say would be
of no importance.
                        I would be gay, I would
(pretend to) kiss. His anger, in childhood,
        had propelled me outward,
to seek a world where to be what he was not,
whatever that might be, might be wanted —
not learned, because I thought I had it in me —
some secret soul yet daunted by his look,
        by his repeated rebuke,
horrified that I might be that way.

How far I ran from him to discover a place
        (New York)
where I could finally begin. Combed my hair
to let it fall over my brow, widened, with effort,
my smile. Especially in snapshots.

I am trying to tell all this too quickly,
as if the right word (that might come to me
as I thought my soul would come to me
as a teenager, breaking away from him) might tell
some truth about us. About him & me.

2. COOLGREANY WOOD

Thoughts of death walking through old oak wood
much of which had been cut for furniture.
Look at a space between branches: no world,
nothing surrounding, clouds indifferent.

Odd affection for the openness of that sky —
Felt his co-presence sharp again within me —
This time it was the universe's turn
　　to say nothing.

At Andy's

for Andy and Martina

Terrace '97. I arrive here on the bus, Andy & Martina pick
me up (while I'm writing I'll try to ignore undercurrents
of the brain, personal worthiness, outcome or 'point' of
this writing, e.g., or should I include them? A pointless
paragraph. I can't write.

OK, I guess I really do have to freewrite & quit fucking
around. So — dive in — splash — *in medias res* — don't
like this pen, point too short — I arrive on the bus —
strip mall on Keith — we stop at Safeway for groceries —
obesity — almost everyone too big, I think, is the weight of
all that food that gets here, by truck (less waste, and, Andy
reminds me, heat loss) added to the bodies of those living
here, Terraceites?

Streets jammed with cars, we take the long way to the
bench, a kid pulling away from the West Side food store
drinking a Coke seems enclosed in his car — encased —

What's wrong is somehow I think there's something to
write *about* — instead of writing.

I'm sitting down here in Andy's basement at Vicky's old
desk on a hot Sunday in August thinking I should write
about something, or rather, that I should (emphasize
should) write (emphasize *write*) to justify my existence
— my life — to myself (& then having justified self, I can
be with others, have a drink with Andy, e.g., without
feeling self-unjustified (un-self-justified?). I'm appalled —
horrified — that at age 63 I still think this way — write
this way. I can't write, Barry & I say. What would 'writing'
be? I think of the quick, sharp (objectivist) takes on heart

169

& world in GB's 'Blondes on Bikes' — I can't do that —
wouldn't even try, to act so nonchalant, i.e., pretend to.
I started out to write about Terrace & here I am writing
about myself, with as bad a fit between this so-called
writing activity (free writing — what's *free* about it?) — &
content — & poetry! — as ever. I should *pray*, I guess —
just keep writing this silly shit & pray for a poem.

•

White hair on the back of my hand — radio going upstairs
— I go upstairs, Andy tells me about constant noise
from next door subdivision — rottweilers, dachshund —
bulldozer — angry crows. I go outside, sit on porch, hear
crows —

I hear crows in Vancouver — I have nothing to write
about, & am not in right state to dive deep — on edge here
— hate this pen — there is no content — or is age content?
(Kavanagh: 'they know it to a day') — fuck that — feeling
myself breathe — insect makes wide sweep around
flowerpot — Teddy barks —

Poetry means (a) I'm going to die — & (b) this notebook
will be read by someone who will see how lacking I am
— unless I destroy it — & I can't do that — that would
be worse than keeping it — that would mean thinking
of it. Better this shit than nothing, better be sitting on
Andy's front porch with Teddy, imagining this shit being
(miraculously) turned into a poem — as Spicer said, not
the Vietnam War but Autumn in Vermont — a poem
about obesity, cheerful obesity, all the big people trundling
their carts & bags of groceries out to their cars parked
at the mall — one lifestyle — nothing but the economy
— the drinking water sour — environmental movement
focused on the immediate, daily threats to health —

At the college — MACLABUSE, one word, becomes
MACL ABUSE, a new threat? Abuse, abuse, obese —
truckloads of log corpses from farther & farther away,
up the Nass — operate the mill at lower cost, develop
the mining sector, truckloads of food — this is a site
of conversion, realization of surplus value, how else to
conceive of it.

No way to conceive of it, no understanding. And I'll never
know if it's really understanding that's disappearing or am
I just moaning the loss of a sharper mind.

Well, I've started writing again.

•

Drinking water — foul — a sour or flat taste & then a
chemical aftertaste — two-stage foulness.

Sky overcast — air muggy — due to automobiles? Is
anything 'natural' anymore?

This is not poetry. But what would a poem about Terrace
be like? Objective — at a distance from the mind, posing
as anybody's perception, idea — or no one's. The View
from Nowhere. But is there another alternative? Ah,
inspiration!

I wish I had a desk — I'm sitting on this duvet in Annyha's
bedroom, balancing the writing book on my naked knees
— I feel like I'm in the jungle. But nothing to pounce on
me, except myself — always pouncing.

Fine rain, and now, to the west, a rift of blue like a river in
the white cloud — blue rifts opening up over the cedars
— fine rain — me here — a visitor — seeing Terrace

171

from the ouside. I was extracted — like a tooth — early retirement — & the skin of Terrace closed easily behind me, the placidity, the obesity. A feeling of contentment — & exclusion — at the edges of this the trees are eaten — the best logs hauled, the second best burned or buried — hauled back here — then the conversion begins — the logs turn into money (the computer watches the saw) — some of it stays here — & then the trucks come, the food — & also the car carriers (any name for that?), rattling & clanking, steel ramps, chains — an objective poem, no one's vision —

Cars moving slowly up Lakelse — cumbersome — in & out of parking spaces — slow — because so heavy & so dangerous — & there is food, in bags, in carts, lifted into trunks & back seats of cars, backs of pickups, in mall lot. Cars & trucks move slowly, heavily, toward the exit, then move like heavy tanks into the traffic lanes, & then, inside all this, inside the cars (the objective poem sees) there are people, placid, cheerful —

What a vision! — is there behind this some animus — is it deep dislike of these people, misanthropy, or just objective — is this a phenomenon anyone could observe or the twisted vision of a fucked-up old man — is there anything natural — or is it *all* natural — blameless — the programmed activities of sapiens with their tree trunks on trucks, wood chips in hopper cars, cars & carts & such no less than insects with sticks & leaves — each has its function, its social role.

The salt lost its savour, but is it only in my life? What is it I don't grant to them, the Terraceites of '97 — the right to be fat & happy & to have overcome (not individually, but *en masse*), simply by not learning it, dread?

172

•

Who can see the inner Terrace? Do our individual
hearts meet there as our social selves meet here in this
slow moving jumble of steel carapaces & Safeway carts
& fat pleasant faces with the log trucks an undertone
in the background? We aren't crowded together there,
that I know. Or do we not meet? Is there a place, even in
summer, where each man (& woman) moves continually
away, through a personal winter, saying, 'this is true'?

There's no way to know except by knowing them, which
here I don't except my old friends —& their knowledge of
each other, seen in faces & heard in tones of voice more
than in words — knowledge of what is not said, out of
kindness — life a condition of unsaying, of waiting for
the unsaid to fade, of waiting for forgetfulness while
preserving shards of memory, of avoiding laying it all on
each other, out of forbearance.

In Hawthorne's story, *The Minister's Black Veil*, the minister
blames his community for their forbearance as if that were
a sin of secrecy & not a balm of love — to suffer the unsaid
in privacy — in one's knowledge that ultimately that's
what there is — aloneness — the urge to lay it all on the
other being a desparate cry, a try, at leaping that bulwark
of loneness, to enforce mutual knowledge, mutual terror.

Do we consume merely out of duty, is it a façade, that we
pretend to savour the objects we devour, pretend to praise
the process, and these fat smiles are not of satisfaction in
consuming but of living in virtue, of never revealing, of
ever concealing, the true life we know the other also lives
— in darkness, in winter?

173

•

(At Mr. Mike's)

I can't separate my feelings from their faces. If I could peel them back like a film, from the fat & placid — huge man ordering grapefruit juice — 'on a diet' — what would they seem?

They would seem nothing — their faces are in my mind — that's not solipsism, just Terrace-ism. I sit in Mr. Mike's — the veggie burger & Coke — a sketch in the brain —

•

(On the Halliwell bus)

The bus driver said of one of his passengers: 'When she started riding the bus she wouldn't say a word. You'd ask her a question & she'd give you just a little short answer. But now . . .' (Pause.) 'She's a Christian, her parents brought her up to be a Christian — but I told her, hey, I don't hold it against you, & she gave a little laugh.'

By which they know how they feel — she knows he didn't mean to dis her faith — but they say so little — 'she wouldn't say a word' means a feeling that could be explained in other words, shy, frightened even, but the driver doesn't —

Maybe the bus driver knows why she wouldn't say a word — abuse — but won't say, maybe because he's protecting her — from a word, spoken out loud, to a stranger — to me — 'I haven't seen you on this bus before' —

Feelings are there in the air, in the mind — 'this side of
the grass' we walk among feelings — & carry feelings in
our brains — & so the faces act as doors — set in lines —
not to let words in. Words dart about inside, puckish —
Andy's father asked what that word meant — mischievous,
méchant — up to no good — words, like spirits, neither
good nor evil, just natural — but some would call them
good *and* evil — Christians — so the faces —

•

Who am I, a ghost? Walking up from Greig to Lakelse —
one of those streets east of Kalum — empty lots & broken
house foundations — weeds — think, am I here — am
I a ghost? I'm not here, not in the sense that thoughts &
feelings & the odd word (at the joint — words at the joints)
would carry me — to the next meeting — I could be going
to a meeting (come in late, like Ken Belford) — for city
politics or to get drunk or for sex — yes, many of those
meanings — meetings — but no network —

& love, & courage, Simon Thompson said, at the bar,
at Hanky's — we had met there every year & now were
meeting again — Rocque, José, Andy — those narratives,
Simon said, are somehow replaced or annihilated — by
consumer —

Happy to read an account of Margaret Laurence's suicide
— her own account — she couldn't find the teakettle to
heat the water to melt the Diazepam — tranquilizer, Andy
says, like Prozac — so she used the coffeemaker, but didn't
put any coffee — just hot water & Prozac — & the glinting
memory — faces of joy — one last?

•

Dream poem: tyler alters / night amber / with sensation.

•

The same world for me as for Andy — we agree. Not the
Thing-in-Itself — that horror-movie creature — but a
thing between us and the Thing — something we have
made up (using all our unspoken language) — call it
world. So how is it I stand in it, on the broken asphalt &
concrete sidewalks of Terrace, & feel it not — feel it *as* not
— as departure, Rilke might say? At Andy's I feel part of
it, hearing Andy's lawnmower, seeing the grey pile rug &
blond dresser in Annyha's room, two pairs of my shoes —
writing at 3:15 p.m. — it feels like I'm here, & that I won't
leave.

The world that seems so frightening (admit it) when
smoking dope (it's the fright I'm admitting, not the dope)
or when thinking — too rationally — you could sit on
the porch — *and* imagine it — stars coming on in the 10
o'clock evening, maybe Orion, time of year? — but chill,
too early for stars to come out fully — late by the clock, but
too early for the meteor shower — Andy's voice from the
dark, down by the barn — 'take 15 or 20 minutes longer,
but I'm not waiting, I'm going to bed.' 'Me too.'

Located in it — not located — in it — not in it — it — not
it — I? — no, not I — the? The the (Barry's line, from
Wallace Stevens). The with stars.

•

Old Lakelse Lake Road — driving to John & Larisa's for
dinner. I'm holding the dessert in my lap — a cake — &
Martina in front of me holds a bowl of caramel sauce.
Andy drives. Dark sky — scattered rain — second growth

176

cedars packed in — roadside bushes — branches waving in the wind. I watch the raindrops crawl up the windshield & I feel the void, like a natural phenomenon, stabbing out of the clouds, or flashing without light — but alternating — on & off — with its absence — something more substantial? — faith?